RESTORATION

RESTORATION

God's Call to the 21st-Century World

PATRICK Q. MASON

Copyright © 2020 Patrick Q. Mason

All rights reserved. No part of this book may be reproduced
or used in any manner without the prior written permission of the copyright
owner, except for the use of brief quotations in a book review.

To request permissions, contact the publisher at info@faithmatters.org.

Paperback: 978-1-953677-04-4
Audiobook: 978-1-953677-06-8
Ebook: 978-1-953677-05-1

Library of Congress Control Number: 2020948308

First edition October 2020.

Printed in the United States of America.

Faith Matters Publishing
2929 W Navigator Drive
Suite 400
Meridian, ID 83642

faithmatters.org

That every [person] might speak in the name of God the Lord, even the Savior of the world;
That faith also might increase in the earth;
That mine everlasting covenant might be established;
That the fulness of my gospel might be proclaimed by the weak and the simple unto the ends of the world . . .

—Doctrine and Covenants 1:20–23

to the glass darklies

Contents

Chapter One: The Fortress Church 1

Chapter Two: Restoring the People of God 11

Chapter Three: Singing a New Song. 25

Chapter Four: The True Church 39

Chapter Five: Excess Baggage 55

Chapter Six: To Renovate the World 73

Appendix: A Restoration Manifesto 91

Acknowledgments 99

CHAPTER ONE

The Fortress Church

In early 2015, my wife, Melissa; three young children (at the time); and I moved to Romania for five months. We had never been there and didn't speak a word of the language. The language barrier made it especially interesting when I was called to be the branch president—my main qualification being my possession of a Y chromosome and hence the Melchizedek Priesthood. I in turn called Melissa to be a Gospel Doctrine teacher. It's amazing how much gospel doctrine you can teach using hand gestures and drawings on a white board.

We lived in the city of Timișoara, in the far west of the country, home of the revolution that in December 1989 toppled dictator Nicolae Ceaușescu. Romania is one of eastern Europe's relatively undiscovered gems, and we loved traveling around the country, taking in both its natural beauty and cultural heritage. One of our most memorable trips was to the Transylvanian village of Viscri. Melissa usually plans our trips, but I was in charge of this one. So when we turned off the main highway onto a "road" apparently going nowhere, with no signs, and taking us past the shabbiest Roma (gypsy) camp we had seen in the country (and we had seen many), I'll confess to being a little nervous.

Fortunately for the safety of our persons and our marriage, after several miles of what became rather charming countryside, we finally stumbled upon the village. Travel websites had advertised Viscri as one of the country's hidden treasures, and it lived up to the billing. We ended up having a marvelous stay, feeling like we were transported back to the fourteenth century (but with running water, electricity, delicious food, and no plague . . . so not really like the fourteenth century at all). We dined in a villager's home, visited a working blacksmith shop, rode on the back of a hay wagon, and scratched our initials into roof tiles shaped from red clay harvested from the earth by the armful.

At the center of the village, like any good European village, is the church. But this is no ordinary church. Elevated on a hill is one of Transylvania's famous fortified Saxon churches, which has been designated a UNESCO World Heritage Site. Dating back to the twelfth century, the white-walled and red-roofed church was where villagers would gather not only for worship but also for safety when marauders came. Indeed, from the outside it looks more like a castle, with narrow window slits, tall towers, and a sturdy wooden gate. This being Romania, there were no guides and no roped-off areas, so we had a grand adventure climbing the parapets, traversing the narrow and rickety wooden walkways, shooting imaginary arrows at imaginary invaders, and trying to keep the kids reverent in the chapel.

Viscri's fortified church is impressive, beautiful, quaint—and totally irrelevant to modern life. The church's main contribution to the twenty-first-century world is as a museum. You go there to be transported briefly into the remote past, not to be guided in your present or future course.

Our Fortress Church

In response to the very real persecution they had received in the nineteenth century, our people—the Latter-day Saints—metaphorically built a fortress church in order to protect ourselves and our precious holdings from invaders. When viewed through narrow arrow slits, the rest of humanity and their ideas—or simply "the world," as we came to know it—seemed ominous and threatening, single-mindedly focused on our destruction. So we closed the gates, occasionally cracking them open to send out missionaries and conduct business, and watched nervously for the next assault.

This isn't meant by way of indictment. I grew up within the walls of the fortress church. It was and is a good place to be. Some of my best memories and most important life lessons came inside the fortress. This is where I learned that I'm a child of Heavenly Parents, that Jesus Christ loves me and died for me, that I can receive personal revelation through the Holy Ghost, and that God still talks to the world through prophets and scriptures meant for our day. As important as the truths I learned inside the fortress church were the values I inherited: faith, love, service, honesty, integrity, forgiveness, sacrifice, family, and community. In my estimation there is nowhere better to gain these attributes than inside the church, and so my wife and I are consciously raising our children within its walls.

Are there really invaders out there? To some degree, yes. The church has always had its critics and enemies. Over the past half century, they have ranged from some (not all) evangelical Christians to some (not all) feminists and gay-rights activists. From inside the fortress, it seemed like other people were always thinking and talking about us. It was easy to suppose that the relatively few raiders who did attack our fortress walls were representative of the whole outside world. And so feeling under siege, we pulled up the bridges and shored up the walls. We looked out from our ramparts with a mixture of pride and disdain . . . and allowed the world to pass us by.

In short, we were becoming quaint. So quaint, in fact, that Broadway produced a smash hit musical about us. Actually, it wasn't really about us, not in any meaningful way. *The Book of Mormon* musical debuted in 2011 not as a testament to our people's ongoing relevance, but rather to the way we had come to stand, in the eyes of theater-goers, for a kind of out-of-time naivete. Our people, ideas, and sacred books were earnest yet ultimately nonthreatening relics, removed from a world that had moved on.

In addition, by the opening decades of the twenty-first century, internal signs appeared suggesting that not all was well in Zion. Our remarkable missionary program had slowed, even stalled, in many corners of the world. With fewer and fewer people listening, the members of our ever-larger missionary force sometimes wondered what exactly they were doing out there. Those eighteen or twenty-four months were a "good learning experience," to be sure, but did they make a real difference to other people? Inside the church, we were losing members, many because they perceived as many problems within the walls of the fortress church as outside. Some experienced the church as a place of spiritual harm, not healing. Many became disenchanted after listening to podcasts or reading a single (long) letter that parroted back the logic and sensibilities of the fortress church. It didn't matter that these critics basically held up the church to a fun house mirror to reveal and exaggerate its most unseemly elements while hiding the parts that were still working wonders for millions. A new generation struggled to maintain interest in the old stories and old ways because we weren't even asking, let alone answering, their current questions. Worst of all, some people—too many—tragically threw themselves off the walls; they had come to believe there was no place for them inside the fortress church but were unable to imagine life outside.

As we commence the third century since God and Jesus Christ appeared to Joseph Smith in the grove, it's important to account for what we've been storing and protecting in the fortress church's treasury all these years. Our personal and collective testimonies of God's love, Christ's Atonement, and the Restoration of the gospel are the crown jewels that must be constantly protected and polished. But in addition to these treasures of inestimable value, when we look around we might also discover a few items gathering dust. A four-hundred-year-old translation of the Bible that wasn't even ours? Stories about our own past that were incomplete and sometimes misleading? Views about the natural world and science that we borrowed from Protestant fundamentalists? Statements about women and racial minorities that, let's just say, haven't aged particularly well? An approach to religious education presuming that God hadn't shed any light on the rest of the world for a millennium and a half? Pedagogies that looked like the game of *Jeopardy!*, where the only acceptable questions were those in which the answer was already given?

In our people's history, there have been moments when the most expedient thing to do was to retreat into the fortress and raise the drawbridge. Having been hounded by mobs, our pioneer forebears thought they could outrun the world. The world caught up. Then they figured they could sequester themselves in their mountain valleys. The world intruded. If physical separation wasn't possible, they surmised, then spiritual separation might work. But the internet has rendered the fortress's walls permeable and fragile. In our twenty-first century information age, there is nowhere to run, nowhere to hide. "The world," as poet William Wordsworth put it, "is too much with us."[1]

Despite its temporary utility, defensive withdrawal cannot be our long-term mode of operation. Our engagement with the world can't just be limited to making money and converts, nor should our interactions be fearful. As Elder Patrick Kearon asked, "Do we fear the world more than we shape it? Do we let our anxieties prevent us from making a difference? Do we spend more time hiding from society's flaws than fixing its problems?" In answer to these searching questions, Elder Kearon concluded, "Society is not something that just happens to us; it is something we help shape. The main thing is to engage, dialogue, bridge, and interact with people of all sorts. Unless we participate, we lose our ability to both influence the world and learn from it."[2] Yes, the Lord counseled his Saints in the last days to "go ye out from among the wicked" and by so doing "save yourselves."[3] It's necessary but not sufficient to save ourselves. Christians in every age have also been called to be the "little yeast" that "leavens the entire lump" and makes it "new."[4] As Joseph Smith taught, a person "filled with the love of God" is not content simply to bless and save their own family and friends, "but ranges through the whole world, anxious to bless the whole of the human family."[5] Having flourished in our fortress, the Restoration's third century is our time to range widely in the world, to both learn from and contribute to it.

Light, Yeast, and Salt

The first line of the church's Bicentennial Proclamation to the World on the Restoration of the Fulness of the Gospel of Jesus Christ, issued by the First Presidency and Council of the Twelve Apostles in April 2020, reads, "We solemnly proclaim that God loves His children in every nation of the world."[6] The Restoration begins with this simple but profound truth: our Heavenly Parents love all their children, everywhere. The Restoration is a divine endowment designed to bless all of humanity.

This expansive vision is central to the Restoration's message, but it can also be a trap. A year and a half after Joseph Smith organized the church, God sent a revelation that announced, "The keys of the kingdom of God are committed unto man on the earth, and from thence shall the gospel roll forth unto the ends of the earth, as the stone which is cut out of the mountain without hands shall roll forth, until it has filled the whole earth."[7] This metaphor has led many interpreters, from Joseph Smith to the present, to believe that the Church of Jesus Christ of Latter-day Saints was destined for numerical greatness. The church's rapid expansion in the second half of the twentieth century led one non-LDS sociologist to predict that the church might boast upwards of a quarter *billion* members by the end of the twenty-first century. In an oft-reprinted claim, this widely respected scholar declared that Mormonism (as he called it) "stands on the threshold of becoming the first major faith to appear on earth since the prophet Muhammad rode out of the desert."[8]

Not only have the growth curves failed to keep up with the exuberant expectations of the 1980s and 1990s, but grandiose images of religious empire and conquest run contrary to the spirit of the gospel of Christ and the nature of the Restoration. When seeing the future church of the Lamb of God in a vision, Nephi beheld that "its numbers were few . . . and their dominions upon the face of the earth were small."[9] How can this be if the kingdom of God is destined to fill the whole earth? As always, Jesus points the way. The metaphors he used to describe his disciples, both ancient and modern, were light, yeast, and salt.[10] Particles of light are so small they are invisible, but they overpower the darkness. Other ingredients are far more substantial, but it's the tiny amount of yeast that causes a lump of dough to rise. And only a pinch of salt transforms a dish from bland to savory.

We are not called to trade our fortress church for a religious empire. Rather, we are called to be light, yeast, and salt—to overpower darkness, elevate the whole, and transform the world. To fill the world with our influence, not necessarily our size. Our dominions will be small, but our reach will be lengthened because we will hold up the Light of the World and by extension become lesser lights shining forth in the darkness.

Jesus doesn't do moats, or drawbridges, or walls. (He does do gates, but only by way of getting us through the right one.[11])

Instead, our Savior is in the business of breaking down walls and building bridges:

> But now in Christ Jesus you who once were far off have been brought near by the blood of Christ. For he is our peace; in his flesh he has made both groups into one and has broken down the dividing wall, that is, the hostility between us. . . . So he came and proclaimed peace to you who were far off and peace to those who were near.[12]

To those inside and outside the dividing wall of the fortress church, Jesus proclaims peace. He replaces hostility with healing. He is the great commissioner of truth and reconciliation. In his flesh and his blood, shared weekly within the body of his church, Christ promises the whole world peace. The Restoration is one way that God sheds his love upon his children in modern times. You and I, "the weak and the simple," are the particles of light, pinches of yeast, and grains of salt through which he will do his "marvelous work."[13]

The Spirit is breathing new life into Christ's church. You can feel it. It's time to lower the drawbridge, open the shutters, and let the air in. It's time to take the precious gifts that God has entrusted us with, and that we have been carefully stewarding for two centuries, and use them to bless the world. It's time to let the Restoration do its work not just for the church but for the world.

The Restoration is God's ongoing invitation to modern humanity to come to Christ and be healed. The Restoration is the work of a loving Father and Mother who are pained that their children needlessly suffer and who have already prepared the banquet for their beloved prodigals. The Restoration is today's fulfillment of an age-old promise to a worldwide family. The Restoration is God's call to our twenty-first-century world.

NOTES

1. William Wordsworth, "The World Is Too Much with Us," https://www.poetryfoundation.org/poems/45564/the-world-is-too-much-with-us, accessed 15 April 2020.

2. Elder Patrick Kearon, "Of Rights and Responsibilities: The Social Ecosystem of Religious Freedom," address delivered at Religious Freedom Annual Review, Brigham Young University, 19 June 2019, accessed 13 July 2020.

3. Doctrine and Covenants 38:42.

4. 1 Corinthians 5:6–7, in Thomas A. Wayment, *The New Testament: A Translation for Latter-day Saints: A Study Bible* (Provo and Salt Lake City, UT: Religious Studies Center and Deseret Book Co., 2019).

5. Letter from Joseph Smith to the Quorum of the Twelve, 15 December 1840, p. 2, The Joseph Smith Papers, https://www.josephsmithpapers.org/paper-summary/letter-to-quorum-of-the-twelve-15-december-1840/2, accessed 13 July 2020.

6. The First Presidency and the Council of the Twelve Apostles of the Church of Jesus Christ of Latter-day Saints, "The Restoration of the Fulness of the Gospel of Jesus Christ: A Bicentennial Proclamation to the World," April 5, 2020, https://www.churchofjesuschrist.org/study/manual/the-restoration-of-the-fulness-of-the-gospel-of-jesus-christ/a-bicentennial-proclamation-to-the-world?lang=eng.

7. Doctrine and Covenants 65:2.

8. Rodney Stark, *The Rise of Mormonism*, ed. Reid L. Neilson (New York: Columbia University Press, 2005), 139.

9. 1 Nephi 14:12.

10. See Matthew 5:13–14; 13:33.

11. See Matthew 7:13.

12. Ephesians 2:13–14, 17 (NRSV).

13. Doctrine and Covenants 1:23; 4:1.

CHAPTER TWO

Restoring the People of God

"Restoration" is one of those terms that only makes sense when connected to something else. In other words, for a restoration to happen, *something* has to be restored. So when we talk about the Restoration, what exactly do we think is being restored?

The church's Bicentennial Proclamation to the World offers a helpful synopsis. According to the proclamation, "The Restoration" entails a restored church, restored priesthood authority (including priesthood keys), and the restored gospel, meaning the doctrine and teachings of Jesus Christ and the prophets and apostles throughout the ages. The work of the Restoration is not yet complete but remains ongoing through the gift of continuing revelation. God continues to inspire and guide the apostles he has called to lead the Church of Jesus Christ of Latter-day Saints, which is "Christ's New Testament Church restored."[1]

But here's the funny thing. As far as I've been able to discover, Joseph Smith never talked about a "restored church." Not once. I've scoured both the scriptures he produced and publications in *The Joseph Smith Papers*, which aims to gather and publish every known surviving Joseph Smith document. Except in the historical introductions, which are written by modern scholars and are not part of the original sources, I have not found a single use of the phrases "restored church" or "restoration of the church."

This was more than a little surprising to me. You might even say it came as a revelation.

It turns out that the first time the phrase "restored church" was used in General Conference came in October 1918 in a talk by Elder James E. Talmage.[2] That is, it occurred more than eighty-eight years after the organization of the church in April 1830. Usage of the phrase increased somewhat over the ensuing years until it consistently appeared in Conference talks about thirty times per decade from the 1950s through the 1990s. References to the "restored church" spiked in General Conference during the 2010s, with its relative usage twice that of any previous decade.[3] This is not to say that the concept of a restored church didn't exist among the earliest generation of Latter-day Saints.[4] It's simply to note that the exact phrase "restored church" seems to have gained traction only during our lifetimes.

Of course, that could be chalked up to idiosyncratic phrasing. What about the "restored gospel"? It turns out that the phrase "restored gospel," while considerably more popular than "restored church," also became popular only in the twentieth century. "Restored gospel" appears a mere three times in General Conference addresses prior to 1900. Even then, it remained only a modestly useful phrase until this century, when usage shot up significantly.[5] That's the general trend for the term "restoration" as well. It certainly appears in nineteenth-century General Conference talks, but in relatively low frequency, then skyrockets to unprecedented levels in the 1990s, 2000s, and 2010s.[6]

Let's allow that to sink in—that when the earliest generations of Latter-day Saints referred to restoration, they rarely invoked the phrase "restored gospel" and never talked (in so many words) about the "restored church." Yet "restoration" was an important part of their religious vocabulary—the word and its variations appear in more than fifty passages in the Book of Mormon and some two dozen in the Doctrine and Covenants, with hundreds more references in *The Joseph Smith Papers*. So what did Joseph Smith and his contemporaries think the Restoration was restoring?

In a word, Israel.

Wait, what?

Restoring Israel

"Restore" and "restoration" are used in various ways in Latter-day Saint scripture and early church teachings. Sometimes the words are used in prosaic fashion, such as when a deposed leader is "restored" to his rightful place.[7] In several passages they refer to resurrection—the "restoration" of our body in its "perfect frame," spoken of so powerfully by Amulek, Jacob, Alma, and Joseph F. Smith.[8] The prophet Joseph Smith wrote and spoke on multiple occasions about the "restoration of the priesthood," mostly in Nauvoo in connection with the developing theology and ordinances of the temple.[9] But the vast majority of references in scripture and Joseph Smith's teachings are to the restoration of the house of Israel in the last days.

Nephi is the first one (in Restoration scripture) to take up this theme. It makes perfect sense, because his family had recently become part of scattered Israel after leaving Jerusalem and making their way through the wilderness and eventually to the promised land.[10] Nephi therefore leaned heavily on the teachings of Isaiah, the preeminent prophet of Israel's dispersal and promised restoration. Hoping to console his family with the knowledge that their exile would not last forever, Nephi "spake unto them much . . . concerning the restoration of the Jews in the latter days."[11] Jacob picked up right where his older brother left off. The stated purpose of his first recorded sermon is to help his Nephite listeners understand that the scattered remnants of Israel would be "restored to . . . the lands of their inheritance, and shall be established in all their lands of promise."[12] Several hundred years later, the prophet Mormon brackets his account of the resurrected Lord's appearance in the promised land with editorial comments about God "restoring all the house of Jacob unto the knowledge of the covenant that he hath covenanted with them."[13]

Joseph Smith's subsequent revelations and teachings follow a similar pattern. A March 1831 revelation about the last days and the Second Coming declares that "the day of redemption" is connected with "the restoration of the scattered Israel."[14] Tellingly, the only explicit reference to "restoration" in the Articles of Faith comes not in relationship to the principles and ordinances of the gospel, or priesthood authority, or the organization of the church, but rather in the tenth article, which proclaims that Latter-day Saints "believe in the literal gathering of Israel and in the restoration of the Ten Tribes."[15]

An important aspect of these pronouncements about the restoration of the house of Israel is specific prophecies regarding the latter-day restoration of the Lamanites, one of the scattered remnants of Israel. Nephi, Jacob, Enos, Alma, Samuel, and Moroni all wrote or preached powerfully on this theme. Samuel spoke poignantly about how the Lamanites—his own people—would "dwindle in unbelief," but that the Lord through his mercy would one day bring about a "restoration of our brethren, the Lamanites, again to the knowledge of the truth."[16] Nephi had a front-row seat to the breaking off of the Lehites from the main branch of Israel as well as the creation of the Lamanites as a separate subbranch. With those scatterings in mind, he prophesied that the restoration of both the Jews and the Lamanites represented a crucial step toward the anticipated time when "the Lord God shall commence his work among all nations, kindreds, tongues, and people, to bring about the restoration of his people upon the earth."[17]

These scriptural passages about the restoration of Israel and the Lamanites are among the least quoted and discussed among contemporary Latter-day Saints. That wasn't always the case. In fact, the first generation of Saints couldn't stop talking about Israel. One historian found that the restoration of Israel was the number-one theme discussed in the Saints' published literature from 1830 to 1846.[18] When Oliver Cowdery reported what the angel Moroni said to Joseph Smith during their long conversation on the night of September 21, 1823, virtually all of it was dedicated to the theme of the restoration of Israel through the lens of multiple Old Testament prophecies.[19] Sidney Rigdon understood the restoration of the house of Israel to be the single most important project that God was undertaking in the last days.[20] Mentions of Israel's restoration in General Conference declined fairly steadily from a high point in the 1870s to an all-time low in the 2000s.[21] Despite our feasting on the Book of Mormon in unprecedented ways, it seems that over the past century, the restoration of Israel—once a staple of the Latter-day Saint theological diet—got bottled up in a dusty jar at the back of the top shelf.

The Restoration of His People

One thing that great chefs do is bring back old recipes and breathe new life into them for modern tastes. In a religious context, prophets often do a similar thing, retrieving neglected or forgotten aspects of our theology or practice and then using them to call us to a renewed sense of worship and discipleship. One of the hallmarks of President Russell M. Nelson's ministry has been the reintroduction of the language of Israel's restoration and gathering into the Latter-day Saint vocabulary. A persistent theme of his presidency is that the gathering of Israel "is the most important thing taking place on earth today."[22] President Nelson has invited us to delve back into those long-neglected passages of the Book of Mormon with fresh eyes and renewed vigor, reconsidering their insistent message concerning the prophesied restoration of the scattered branches of Israel, including the Lamanites, in modern times.

For many modern readers, the scriptures' talk of "Israel" can seem archaic, even clannish. Furthermore, any Latter-day Saint who has Jewish friends knows how awkward that conversation can be, as if we are appropriating their people's ancient identity and homeland. So how can we be faithful to the prophetic injunction to restore Israel in a way that makes sense in the twenty-first century?

Not surprisingly, given his obsession with the theme, Nephi provides the key. He explains that the restoration of the various branches of Israel—the Jews, the scattered tribes, and the remnant of Lehi—will be accomplished for the sake of God's age-old promises to those particular peoples and also as part of a more general work whereby God will "bring about *the restoration of his people* upon the earth."[23] Similarly, in one of the most important revelations to Joseph Smith about priesthood and missionary work—two of the great tools of the gathering of Israel—the Lord affirms that the church, the words of the prophets, and the gathering of the Saints have all been brought about so as to accomplish one great goal: "*the restoration of his people*."[24]

Put another way, there are many things that have been lost and scattered that need to be restored: Israel, the Lamanites, the gospel, the priesthood, the church, covenants, ordinances, spiritual gifts, and so forth. We call the whole package "the restoration of all things."[25] This all-encompassing phrase originated with Jesus.[26] He in turn was invoking the prophet Malachi, whom Moroni quoted to Joseph Smith, referring to the coming of Elijah in the last days to "turn the heart of the fathers to the children, and the heart of the children to their fathers." In other words, from the Hebrew prophets to Christ, from the Nephite prophets to Joseph Smith and the modern church, the message has been the same. God's great restoration project seeks to unite all generations of the human family from the beginning to the present and onward all the way to the end of time. In fact, as Malachi and Moroni prophesied, without this restoration "the whole earth would be utterly wasted"; all of God's work of creation would in the end come to naught.[27]

Yes, there are many "things" to restore. But ultimately God isn't concerned with restoring "things" as much as he is with using those things to restore what really matters—"his people." So the "restoration of all things" is designed with one grand aim in mind: restoring God's people—our Father and Mother's children, their eternal family—to wholeness.[28]

The restoration of God's people simultaneously affirms and transcends human individuality. We will each be restored to our own families even as we are all reunited with the entire family of God. Isaiah was so concerned about the restoration of the house of Israel because he had the burden of seeing its scattering. Nephi and the subsequent Lehite prophets likewise worried about the scattering and restoration of Lehi's surviving descendants. It was only natural that they would focus their prophecies on the parts of the vineyard they had been specially called to tend. For modern readers of these texts, it is essential that we neither ignore nor co-opt the promises God made to these distinct branches of his family. God made a covenant with Abraham and his descendants whereby not only they but all the people of the earth would be blessed. The Abrahamic covenant was at once particular to the people of Israel and general in its total effect. Similarly, God's promises about the restoration of the Lamanites came in response to their unique situation but were also part of a much broader story about God's redemption of the world.[29] In other words, God will restore the Lamanites—both as Lamanites, with any of the righteous traditions of their mothers and fathers, and as part of the whole human family.

However, most of us are *not* Israel, not in the original sense, nor are we Lamanites. We are recipients or inheritors of God's promises to Abraham, not necessarily by virtue of biological descent but rather as the effects of those promises ripple across time and throughout the human family. One of the key innovations of Christian theology, originally formulated by the apostle Paul, is that those who believe and are baptized in the name of Jesus become *adopted* into a new Israel and therefore live a new life under a new covenant. This is the teaching of the modern church as well, which affirms with Paul that we "are all the children of God by faith in Christ Jesus. . . . And if ye be Christ's, then are ye Abraham's seed, and heirs according to the promise."[30] In short, God's promises to original Israel and new Israel are remarkably similar. Each of us stands to inherit all the blessings of Abraham, no matter where we fit on the family tree or how we got there. The purpose of the Restoration is to fulfill the ancient promises that all of God's children, regardless of the nation or clan they find themselves born into, can and will be "heirs to the kingdom of God."[31]

The Holiest Objects

One of the things I love about studying history is that it enables me to learn about and enter into the experiences of people whose lives are totally different from my own upbringing as a white male Latter-day Saint in a middle-class suburb of Salt Lake City. Although I can learn from and appreciate other people's stories, there is a certain violence in claiming them as my own. For instance, I have posters of Martin Luther King Jr. and Malcolm X hanging on the wall in my office because they have deeply shaped my own ethical formation and how I see the world. As much as I study about African American lives and histories, however, their story isn't my story. This is true especially because their collective identity has been shaped by an experience of shared suffering that I simply do not, and never can, inhabit.

Similarly, the stories of original Israel and the Lamanites are, to a significant degree, stories of suffering. As their histories played out, both peoples were scattered, despised, persecuted, marginalized, and they dwindled. In the Book of Mormon, the prophet Jacob taught that God would be especially merciful toward the people the Nephites regarded as "filthy."[32] God's word holds out special promises for the Lamanites because God's heart beats in sympathy with his oppressed and marginalized children. It is no coincidence that when Jesus announced his atoning ministry and first proclaimed his messiahship, he quoted from Isaiah, the great prophet of Israel's scattering and restoration:

> The Spirit of the Lord is upon me, because he hath anointed me to preach the gospel to the poor; he hath sent me to heal the brokenhearted, to preach deliverance to the captives, and recovering of sight to the blind, to set at liberty them that are bruised.[33]

The poor. The brokenhearted. The captives. The blind. The bruised. These are the people to whom the Messiah's anointing is directed. On a spiritual level, that could be anyone. But in a historical sense, Jesus's words apply directly to Israel, the Lamanites, and every other subjugated and victimized people. Our God, the Messiah of the marginalized, "will swallow up death in victory; and the Lord God will wipe away tears from off all faces; and the rebuke of his people shall he take away from off all the earth."[34] In other words, he will restore Israel, he will restore the Lamanites, and he will restore all "his people."

Any restoration we claim to participate in must therefore be primarily oriented toward those who have suffered on the margins of history and currently suffer on the margins of society. The Saints of the nineteenth and twentieth centuries felt confident about where and how to find scattered Israel and the Lamanites. In this century we have become humbler about our ability to identify precisely who is in each group. If we presume that the ten tribes of Israel are still by and large lost, and if because of DNA testing we no longer have confidence in who or where the descendants of the Lamanites are, then to some significant degree I think we have to leave it directly in the Lord's hands to bring about those particular restorations.[35] That leaves us with the task of restoring to wholeness those children of God in our contemporary world whose experiences are primarily those of suffering and marginalization—those in whom we can hear the echoes and see the image of original Israel and the Lamanites. Those who are despised, and rejected, and scattered. Those who are deemed by some as filthy. Refugees and displaced persons. Immigrants. The poor. The homeless. Racial minorities. Those who suffer from disabilities or mental illness. Victims of physical, sexual, and emotional abuse. That's where God's particular work of restoration will happen today, as part of the general restoration of all his people.

The great Christian author C. S. Lewis beautifully wrote that "next to the Blessed Sacrament itself, your neighbor is the holiest object presented to your senses."[36] In Restoration theology, we don't believe in what Catholics and others call the "real presence" of Jesus in our sacramental emblems. Therefore, applying a somewhat revised version of Lewis's profound insight, we can affirm that there is absolutely nothing in this world that is holier than the person next to you. She is not only created in the image of God but has existed with God from the eternities and will continue to do so forever and ever, potentially as a goddess herself. Because of its unique view of who we really are, where we come from, and what we are destined to become, the Restoration must stand at the forefront of the modern commitment to human dignity for all people.

The restoration will remain ongoing and incomplete so long as there are any poor or "any manner of -ites" among us.[37] Zion has not been achieved. Followers of Christ therefore have a special calling to the poor, the brokenhearted, the captives, the blind, the bruised—both our sisters and brothers immediately in our midst as well as those who find themselves in dire circumstances anywhere in the world. In his beautiful discussion of spiritual gifts, Paul reminded the ancient members of the body of Christ that "the members of the body, even though they seem to be weaker, are essential, and those members of the body that seem less honorable, we place greater honor on them." Why do we do this? Because God does. The apostle continues, "God has brought the body together, while giving greater honor to the lesser members."[38] Both individually and communally, we are to live out the parable of the prodigal son.[39]

So what is being restored in the Restoration? God's people. The poor will receive the kingdom of heaven. The brokenhearted will be healed. The captives will be liberated. The blind will see. The bruised will be made whole. In the ultimate sense, this is the work of atonement and reconciliation that only our Savior Jesus Christ can fully accomplish. But in the more immediate sense, the call of the Restoration is for each recipient of Christ's redeeming love to extend that grace by co-participating with him as "saviors . . . on Mount Zion."[40]

That salvation cannot and will not wait for the next world. The restoration of God's people is here. The restoration of God's people is now.

NOTES

1. The First Presidency and the Council of the Twelve Apostles of the Church of Jesus Christ of Latter-day Saints, "The Restoration of the Fulness of the Gospel of Jesus Christ: A Bicentennial Proclamation to the World," April 5, 2020, https://www.churchofjesuschrist.org/study/manual/the-restoration-of-the-fulness-of-the-gospel-of-jesus-christ/a-bicentennial-proclamation-to-the-world?lang=eng.

2. James E. Talmage, address in *Eighty-Ninth Semi-Annual Conference of the Church of Jesus Christ of Latter-day Saints* (Salt Lake City: Deseret News, 1918), 61.

3. Statistical analysis based on https://www.lds-general-conference.org/, keyword search for "restored church."

4. Parley P. Pratt did refer to "the restoration of the Church of God" in 1856, but the particular phrase "restoration of the church" does not reappear in the General Conference record until 1939. Parley P. Pratt, "Progress of the Latter-Day Church – The Saints of All Ages Cooperating for the Success of the Kingdom of God on the Earth," *Journal of Discourses* 3:45 (April 7, 1856).

5. https://www.lds-general-conference.org/, keyword searches "restored gospel" and "restoration."

6. In five different thirty-year generational cohorts from 1830 to 1979, "restoration" was only a top-ten theme once, in the period from 1920 to 1949, when it ranked tenth. And yet the Restoration became one of the most prominent themes in Conference from 1980 to 2009. Gordon Shepherd and Gary Shepherd, *A Kingdom Transformed: Early Mormonism and the Modern LDS Church*, 2nd ed. (Salt Lake City: University of Utah Press, 2016), 73, 76, 216.

7. Alma 62:8; Ether 7:9.

8. Alma 11:44; 2 Nephi 9:12; Alma 40:23; Doctrine and Covenants 138:17. "Restoration" is a particularly prominent theme in Alma's discourse to his son Corianton, with some twenty-seven references in the space of three chapters (Alma 40–42). Most of these references point to the resurrection of the body and the moral state of the soul after resurrection.

9. Doctrine and Covenants 128:17; see also 124:28; 127:8; 132:45.

10. See Terryl Givens, *2nd Nephi: A Brief Theological Introduction* (Provo, UT: Neal A. Maxwell Institute for Religious Scholarship, 2020), 2–7.

11. 1 Nephi 15:19–20.

12. 2 Nephi 9:1–2.

13. 3 Nephi 5:25–26; see also 3 Nephi 29:1; Mormon 5:14.

14. Doctrine and Covenants 45:17.

15. Articles of Faith 1:10.

16. Helaman 15:11.

17. 2 Nephi 30:4–8.

18. Grant Underwood, "Book of Mormon Usage in Early LDS Theology," *Dialogue: A Journal of Mormon Thought* 17:3 (Autumn 1984): 35–74, see especially 39–41.

19. Oliver Cowdery, "Letter VI," *LDS Messenger and Advocate*, Apr. 1835, 1:108–112; reprinted in Karen Lynn Davidson et al, eds., *The Joseph Smith Papers, Histories, Volume 1: Joseph Smith Histories, 1832–1844* (Salt Lake City, UT: The Church Historian's Press, 2012), 64–71, quote from p. 70.

20. Rigdon wrote, "The only thing which God promised to the world, after the great apostacy . . . was to return the scattered remnants of Jacob, and gather the house of Joseph; bringing them as he did at the first, and building them as he did at the beginning." "Millenium No. II," *The Evening and the Morning Star* 2:16 (January 1834), 251.

21. https://www.lds-general-conference.org/, keyword search "Israel"; see also Shepherd and Shepherd, *A Kingdom Transformed*, 286.

22. Russell M. Nelson and Wendy W. Nelson, "Hope of Israel," worldwide youth devotional, 3 June 2018, https://www.churchofjesuschrist.org/study/broadcasts/worldwide-devotional-for-young-adults/2018/06/hope-of-israel?lang=eng. See also Russell M. Nelson, "Sisters' Participation in the Gathering of Israel," October 2018 General Conference, https://www.churchofjesuschrist.org/study/general-conference/2018/10/sisters-participation-in-the-gathering-of-israel?lang=eng.

23. 2 Nephi 30:8, emphasis added.

24. Doctrine and Covenants 84:2, emphasis added.

25. Doctrine and Covenants 27:6; 86:10.

26. Matthew 17:11.

27. Malachi 4:6; Joseph Smith-History 1:36–39.

28. Here I am inspired by, though ultimately going in a somewhat different direction than, Philip L. Barlow, "To Mend a Fractured Reality: Joseph Smith's Project," *Journal of Mormon History* 38:3 (Summer 2012): 28–50.

29. For a more textured reading of Nephi and Isaiah's prophecies about the restoration of Israel, see Joseph Spencer, *1st Nephi: A Brief Theological Introduction* (Provo, UT: Neal A. Maxwell Institute for Religious Scholarship, 2020), chapter 2.

30. Galatians 3:26–29. Joseph Smith believed that those who converted to the church either were already of the literal blood of Israel, or became such through a miraculous transformation wrought by the power of the Holy Ghost. At the same time, adoption into Israel was a common theme in early church teaching. In the contemporary church, no distinction is made between those who may be literal descendants of Israel and those who are adopted into Israel through baptism. See Terryl L. Givens, *Wrestling the Angel: The Foundations of Mormon Thought: Cosmos, God, Humanity* (New York: Oxford University Press, 2015), 168–170.

31. 4 Nephi 1:17.

32. See Jacob 3:6–9.

33. Luke 4:18; see Isaiah 61:1.

34. Isaiah 25:8.

35. Some have supposed that the "gathering of Israel" effected through our church's missionary efforts is a primary means by which scattered Israel is being restored. My sense is that bringing people to Christ through the church is tantamount to gathering them to *new* Israel, which is a different (and equally valid) project than restoring original Israel. For more information on how the findings of modern geneticists led us to change some of our suppositions about Lamanite identity, see "Book of Mormon and DNA Studies," https://www.churchofjesuschrist.org/study/manual/gospel-topics-essays/book-of-mormon-and-dna-studies?lang=eng, accessed 15 July 2020.

36. C. S. Lewis, *The Weight of Glory: And Other Addresses* (San Francisco: HarperCollins, 1949; reprint, 2001), 46.

37. Moses 7:18; 4 Nephi 1:17.

38. 1 Corinthians 12:22–24, in Thomas A. Wayment, *The New Testament: A Translation for Latter-day Saints: A Study Bible* (Provo and Salt Lake City, UT: Religious Studies Center and Deseret Book Company, 2019).

39. See Luke 15:11–32.

40. Obadiah 1:21.

CHAPTER THREE

Singing a New Song

Back when I was a missionary, we introduced the concepts of the Restoration to investigators during the third discussion. We were always very happy to get to this lesson because it meant that the person hadn't told us to scram after the second discussion, at the end of which we asked them to get baptized. The third lesson itself was basically a historical narrative: During his mortal ministry, Jesus Christ established his church led by his chosen twelve apostles. After the apostles' deaths, there was an apostasy, which led to a loss of truth and priesthood authority, which necessitated a restoration of those things that were lost. This restoration of truth and authority came about in modern times through the calling of the prophet Joseph Smith; the restoration of the priesthood at the hands of John the Baptist and Peter, James, and John; and the restoration of the true Church of Jesus Christ . . . which, you'll remember, we just asked you to get baptized into.

I typically supplemented the official teaching material with an analogy, no doubt inherited from some MTC teacher or senior companion:

"Imagine you have a beautiful table with a glass top. Then imagine your tabletop breaks, with its shards scattering all over the place. Some pieces you can find but don't know how to put back together the right way, and others are lost altogether. It's a mess, and you can't simply look at the original assembly instructions and glue the table back together. You've got to *restore* it, which means getting a new table top that looks and performs just like the old one. And the only way to ensure you've got the right tabletop, which fits perfectly just like the old one, is to get it from the original manufacturer."

Okay, so it's not the best church metaphor you've ever heard—but admit it, it's not the worst either.

One of the key takeaways of the discussion was supposed to be that the church Joseph Smith organized in 1830 wasn't a new thing but rather the restoration of a very old thing. Mind you, it wasn't just a *reformation*, as we were eager to point out—the tabletop is hopelessly broken (cough, Catholics, cough), and you can't just glue it back together because a bunch of the pieces are lost (cough, Protestants, cough). In other words, the third discussion provided a theological narrative designed to address a very particular set of questions, which happen to be the same questions that Joseph Smith had as a fourteen-year-old boy: "which of all the [Christian] sects was right . . . and which I should join." The answer that Jesus gave in the grove, and that we've been giving ever since, is "none of them."[1] Hence the need for a *restored* Church of Jesus Christ.

Growing up in the church, I was taught—and in turn taught others—that the Restoration entailed bringing back something old. In this view, the Church of Jesus Christ of Latter-day Saints is the functional equivalent of a contemporary staging of a Shakespeare play in a carefully and lovingly restored version of the Globe Theater. The performance features modern actors and sets, of course, but we also have the comfort of knowing that it's the same old classic Bard as performed in the "original" setting. We can call this perspective the "Restoration-as-reprise." That view has been affirmed by many leaders of the church, and it certainly resonates with my love for history. I still believe it's a true story in many important respects.

But we miss something beautiful, profound, and important about the Restoration when we think about it only as a reprise of an original melody, or the remastering of a classic recording, or the reboot of an obsolete TV show we used to love before it went away. Perhaps we have focused so much on the primitivist elements of the Restoration—those aspects that hark back to an earlier age—that we have overlooked some of its prophetic power for today.

That is to say, what if the Restoration isn't meant to get us to look *backward* as much as it is to get us to look *forward*? We don't have to deny the essential connection to previous dispensations—this is not a matter of either-or. But something remarkable can happen when we emphasize the "new" in the "new and everlasting covenant," when we believe that God isn't just singing old standards, but continuously composing new melodies and laying down new beats in order to capture the ears and hearts of new generations. There's nothing shameful about playing in a tribute band that dutifully rehearses familiar oldies, albeit to dwindling crowds. But what would it be like to be in the studio alongside our Frontman, actively co-creating with him as he composes and records a "new song" for a contemporary audience?[2] What would it mean to make the Restoration as new and relevant in 2020 (and every year thereafter) as it was in 1820?

Old Things Pass Away, and All Things Are Made New

The notion of Restoration-as-reprise stretches back to the formative years of the church. Specifically, the idea was introduced through the influence of prominent early converts such as Sidney Rigdon and Parley P. Pratt. Rigdon had spent the 1820s as a pastor in various Baptist churches and was a key contributor to the restorationist movement led by Alexander Campbell. The "Campbellites," as they were known prior to becoming a formal denomination called the Disciples of Christ, believed that the Christian churches of the day had deviated from biblical purity and needed to be restored to the original form as outlined in the New Testament. The popular notion of "restorationism" was already in the air before 1830. Indeed, many early converts joined the church founded by Joseph Smith precisely because they believed in the restoration of apostolic authority and spiritual gifts as prophesied in the New Testament.[3]

Like Rigdon, Parley P. Pratt brought into the church his earlier ideas about restorationism. In particular, he believed that God's work of restoration in the last days entailed a return to an earlier state of purity that had subsequently been corrupted. Pratt popularized these views in his 1837 tract *A Voice of Warning*, which, other than the Book of Mormon, was arguably the most influential and widely read Latter-day Saint publication of the entire nineteenth century. According to Pratt, the "restoration of all things" promised in the Bible meant that "all things have undergone a change, and are to be again restored to their primitive order, in which they first existed";[4] scholars call this view "primitivism." For Pratt, restoration was not limited to the structure of the church. Fallen humanity needed to be restored through the resurrection and redemption of Christ, Israel needed to be restored as God's covenant people, and the earth itself needed to be restored to its paradisiacal glory following the Fall. In every case, the present state of affairs was a corrupted downgrade from God's first revelation or creation. The purpose of restoration was therefore to return all things to their pristine original form. In Pratt's estimation, the gospel delivered to Joseph Smith was not new to the nineteenth century but was the latest reprise of a gospel message that had its origins from before the foundations of the world. "We have only the old thing," he proclaimed in 1847, "it was old in Adams day it was old in Mormons day . . . & it was old in 1830 when we first began to preach it."[5]

This primitivist understanding of the Restoration arguably became the dominant one in the church, owing in no small degree to the popularity and effectiveness of *A Voice of Warning*. But there was always another way to think about what began on that spring day in 1820. Joseph Smith himself hinted at this other view, which we might call "Restoration-as-rise," in the opening paragraph of his first recorded history. This 1832 document had a dual purpose—it was intended both as "a History of the life of Joseph Smith Jr." and "an account of the rise of the church of Christ in the eve of time." As Joseph understood it, the rise of the church was built on four pillars: first, "the testimony from on high," presumably referring to the First Vision; second, "the ministering of Angels," probably a reference to Moroni; third, "the reception of the holy Priesthood by the ministering of Angels," no doubt referring to John the Baptist; and fourth, Joseph's "reception of the high Priesthood . . . [and] the Keys of the Kingdom of God" at the hands of Peter, James, and John.[6]

The language here indicates the emergence of something new and distinctive. Joseph refers to the "rise," not the reprise, of the church. Yes, the organization of the church is brought about by the visitation of angels who had walked the earth many centuries before. But these ancients don't try to drag Joseph backward in time—rather, they come bearing gifts of knowledge and authority to the modern world. The Restoration is not about re-entering or re-creating a sacred past, as many primitivists sought to do, but rather summoning the past in the service of a holy present. Joseph sought less to return to Eden than to create an Eden for a new age.

Given his primitivist disposition, it's ironic that perhaps no one captured this distinctly non-primitivist sentiment better than Parley Pratt. In an 1841 editorial in the *Millennial Star*,

Pratt declared that in "the great restoration of all things" God had breathed a new spirit into the world:

> *new* in priesthood, *new* in ordinances, *new* in spirit, gifts, and blessings. . . . In short it is a NEW "TREE"—NEW "FRUITS,"— "NEW CLOTH," and "NEW GARMENTS,"—"NEW WINE" and "NEW BOTTLES"—"NEW LEVEN" and a "NEW LUMP," "a new covenant" and spirit; and may it roll on till we have a new heaven and a new earth, that we may dwell forever in the new Jerusalem, while old things pass away, and all things are made new.[7]

The point could not be clearer: through the Restoration, God is doing a new work in and for a new age. It is a new chapter in salvation history, the latest development in God's everlasting work of redemption. Hence, God's promises offered to humanity through the Restoration are simultaneously "new" and "everlasting."

The Restoration is, in short, a thoroughly modern project, not the mechanical replication of a two-thousand-year-old organizational chart. There's nothing wrong with trying to reproduce the forms of New Testament Christianity, but the Church of Jesus Christ isn't meant to be a glorified archaeological excavation or a living history museum. It must be imbued with new gifts, new blessings, new covenants, and a new spirit—all with the purpose of growing a new tree that will bear new fruits.

This is why rebaptism was necessary for the first members of the church in April 1830. It wasn't because God had shut his eyes to the sincere proclamation of faith as demonstrated in many centuries' worth of Christian sacraments. Rather, God told the fledgling church, it was because "all old covenants have I caused to be done away in this thing; and this is a new and an everlasting covenant." Their previous performances, though not retrospectively condemned, would be considered "dead works" moving forward. Just as Jesus Christ had offered a new covenant when he walked the earth "in days of old," now once again he had "caused this last covenant and this church to be built up unto me."[8]

God hit the reset button. It was time to turn the page, to start anew.

The Ongoing Restoration

A subtle but significant rhetorical shift occurred in the church during the April 2014 General Conference. Almost in passing, Dieter F. Uchtdorf, then Second Counselor in the First Presidency, introduced the notion of an "ongoing" Restoration:

> Sometimes we think of the Restoration of the gospel as something that is complete, already behind us—Joseph Smith translated the Book of Mormon, he received priesthood keys, the Church was organized. In reality, the Restoration is an ongoing process; we are living in it right now. It includes "all that God has revealed, all that He does now reveal," and the "many great and important things" that "He will yet reveal."[9]

In the years that followed, "ongoing Restoration" became something of a buzzword among Latter-day Saints.[10] I don't believe President Uchtdorf intentionally meant to create a new catchphrase or hashtag; indeed, as you can see, he didn't even use that precise wording. Rather, "ongoing Restoration" has become organically popular because it succinctly captures something important about who we are and what we believe.

What began with Joseph Smith was exactly that—a beginning. Then and now, the work of restoration was more about direction than destination.[11] Or, as President Russell M. Nelson observed, the Restoration is a "process" that we are privileged to witness and participate in. "If you think the Church has been fully restored," he said, "you're just seeing the beginning. There is much more to come."[12]

What does it mean to be part of an "ongoing Restoration"? On one level, it's just what President Uchtdorf suggested, namely that as a church with an Article of Faith that embraces the notion of continuing revelation, we see the Restoration as something that is continually unfolding rather than as something already accomplished. Certainly, we build on the insights and achievements of previous generations, but we believe God has more to say—not only because changing circumstances require new responses, but because an eternal God still has much more to teach us. The Restoration is ongoing because God has unfinished business with the world. We don't believe in a Deist Creator who did his part and then left us to our own devices, with the universe running like an intricate clock while he lounges on a beach in some distant corner of the cosmos. Rather, we believe in Heavenly Parents who remain deeply invested and intimately involved in the lives of their children. We worship a personal God who never sleeps, never rests, never takes a day off in pursuing his "work and glory" of enticing his children to share his life with him.[13] The Restoration is the ongoing reconciliation between God and humanity in modern times.

Fundamental to the concept of an ongoing Restoration is ongoing revelation to both individuals and the church as a whole. This gift cannot be minimized, but it's also not meant to be hoarded. As part of our standard apostasy narrative, Latter-day Saints have overgeneralized the response that Joseph Smith received from a Methodist minister upon reporting the details of the First Vision to him. We have supposed that this one preacher's opinion, that "there were no such things as visions or revelations in these days; that all such things had ceased with the apostles, and that there would never be any more of them," represented the view of all Christians in the early nineteenth century and ever since.[14] To the contrary, countless other good women and men have experienced profound visions of God, Jesus, and angels—prior to, at the time of, and since Joseph Smith's transformative visions.[15] Over the centuries and still today, many other Christians have embraced the notion that "God is still speaking."[16] For instance, the outpouring of spiritual gifts so prominent in the early decades of the modern Church of Jesus Christ—healings, visions, tongues, prophesying—are now more commonly displayed among our Pentecostal sisters and brothers than in our own congregations. This is not to say God's power as demonstrated through spiritual gifts is not present among the Latter-day Saints—far from it. It's only to emphasize that our people have no more of a monopoly on ongoing revelation than we do on truth or goodness. After all, we believe that at some future point in the ongoing Restoration, we'll receive (or come to recognize) additional sacred records documenting how God has spoken to "all nations of the earth."[17] Part of our role as agents of the Restoration is to rejoice in God's ongoing revelation, wherever it happens, and to declare to every people in every nation that they have every right to hear God speaking to them "according to their language, unto their understanding."[18] This is good news to proclaim, indeed.

By itself, ongoing revelation is insufficient to fuel an ongoing Restoration—or at least not if we understand revelation simply to be the act of God speaking to his children. As any parent knows, talking *to* your kids is one thing, but it's another thing entirely for them to listen and understand. The gift of ongoing revelation must therefore be paired with the gift of discernment. We have to listen to God's voice and discern what that voice is telling us today.[19] It is not enough to know what God intended for his children only in previous generations, as recorded in the scriptures—though as our "standard works" they are indispensable and timeless guides. We have to know what God wants for us right now.

The ongoing Restoration means that every generation, and every person, must rediscover the gospel of Jesus Christ for themselves. The pioneers' Restoration was for the pioneers. Your grandparents' Restoration was for your grandparents. What does the Restoration mean for you, today, at this moment? What does God need you to do that no other person and no other generation has ever done? Sure, there are plenty of constants across time and space—that's what the first principles and ordinances are, and this is why we always build upon the solid foundation of prophets and apostles with Christ as the chief cornerstone.[20] But what's the "new song" that God wants to write and sing with you? The melody you sing will harmonize with those who have gone before, but it will be yours, not theirs. The church you build and participate in will share much in common with the one your grandparents established, but it has to be yours, not theirs. The church has to be alive, has to breathe, has to keep the faith with the tradition while remaining alive to the present workings of the Spirit.

None of this is to relegate primitivism to the dustbin of history (or theology). At its best, primitivism serves as a prophetic check on the cult of the new. Recall Paul's disgust at the Athenians who "spent their time in nothing else, but either to tell, or to hear some new thing."[21] In both religion and human society, newer isn't always better. There is a reason why one of the most common refrains in the Book of Mormon is to remember the Lord's mercies to his children since the beginning of time. The ongoing Restoration never loses sight of the righteous traditions of our mothers and fathers, and it strives to keep faith with previous generations' faithfulness. At the same time, in the ongoing Restoration we use tradition as a springboard to propel us forward, not as an anchor to keep us stationary.

This is the exciting part. We weren't put on earth to watch reruns, no matter how good those old episodes were. We're not here just to reenact great moments from sacred history. We're here to make something new, and to do it in partnership with God. The ongoing Restoration is the "new" in the "new and everlasting covenant." God calls us to co-create with him, to co-restore with him, until working together we behold a new heaven and a new earth.

NOTES

1. Joseph Smith—History 1:18–19.

2. Psalm 40:3; Doctrine and Covenants 84:98–102.

3. See Terryl L. Givens and Matthew J. Grow, *Parley P. Pratt: The Apostle Paul of Mormonism* (New York: Oxford University Press, 2011), 21–26; Steven L. Shields, "Joseph Smith and Sidney Rigdon: Co-Founders of a Movement," *Dialogue: A Journal of Mormon Thought* 52:3 (Fall 2019): 1–18.

4. P. P. Pratt, *A Voice of Warning and Instruction to All People* (New York: W. Sandford, 1837), 147.

5. Minutes of meeting in Winter Quarters, 25 April 1847, Historian's Office general Church minutes, 1839–1877, Church History Library, available online at https://catalog.churchofjesuschrist.org/assets?id=64dd3c76-edfc-4ed2-8c7c-24d88ce31b07&crate=0&index=28.

6. "History, Circa Summer 1832," in Karen Lynn Davidson et al., eds., *The Joseph Smith Papers, Histories, Volume 1: Joseph Smith Histories, 1832–1844* (Salt Lake City, UT: The Church Historian's Press, 2012), 10, spelling corrected for readability.

7. [Parley P. Pratt,] "Grapes from Thorns, and Figs from Thistles," *The Latter-day Saints' Millennial Star* vol. 1 no. 9 (January 1841): 238, spelling and emphasis as in original. This editorial was reprinted in Nauvoo, with some typographical revisions, in *Times and Seasons*, 15 June 1842.

8. Doctrine and Covenants 22:1–3. It was several years later when Joseph Smith received the revelation instituting baptisms for the dead, which provided a ritual solution to the problem of all those who had lived and died without hearing the gospel or receiving the required authorized ordinances. See Doctrine and Covenants 127 and 128.

9. Dieter F. Uchtdorf, "Are You Sleeping through the Restoration?" *Ensign* (May 2014): 59. President Uchtdorf's comments echoed what Elder Jeffrey R. Holland had previously called, during his very first Conference address as an apostle, "the ongoing saga" and "ongoing miracle of the Restoration." Jeffrey R. Holland, "Miracles of the Restoration," October 1994 General Conference, available online at https://www.churchofjesuschrist.org/study/general-conference/1994/10/miracles-of-the-restoration?lang=eng.

10. For recent usages by General Authorities, see Gary E. Stevenson, "The Ongoing Restoration," BYU Speeches, 20 August 2019; Quentin L. Cook, "Adjustments to Strengthen Youth," *Ensign* (October 2019); LeGrand R. Curtis Jr., "The Ongoing Restoration," *Ensign* (April 2020); Russell M. Nelson,

"The Future of the Church: Preparing the World for the Savior's Second Coming," *Ensign* (April 2020).

11. See LeGrand R. Curtis Jr., "The Ongoing Restoration," *Ensign* (April 2020). Thanks also to Rob Daines for some of this language.

12. "Latter-day Saint Prophet, Wife and Apostle Share Insights of Global Ministry," Newsroom, 30 October 2018, https://newsroom.churchofjesuschrist.org/article/latter-day-saint-prophet-wife-apostle-share-insights-global-ministry, accessed 15 July 2020.

13. Moses 1:39.

14. Joseph Smith–History 1:21.

15. On Joseph Smith's contemporaries, see Richard L. Bushman, "The Visionary World of Joseph Smith," *BYU Studies* 37:1 (1997–98): 183–204.

16. This particular phrase has been a successful campaign by the United Church of Christ since 2004 (see https://www.ucc.org/god-is-still-speaking). For a historical treatment see David F. Holland, *Sacred Borders: Continuing Revelation and Canonical Restraint in Early America* (New York: Oxford University Press, 2011).

17. 2 Nephi 29:12.

18. 2 Nephi 31:3.

19. See Doctrine and Covenants 50:21–22.

20. See Ephesians 2:18–20.

21. Acts 17:21.

CHAPTER FOUR

The True Church

One of the courses I teach at Utah State University is "Religion, Violence, and Peace." A major goal of the course is to introduce students to various religious traditions around the globe. So over the course of several weeks we take a whirlwind tour of Judaism, Christianity, Islam, Buddhism, Hinduism, the Church of Jesus Christ of Latter-day Saints, and indigenous traditions. It's great fun.

I recently had a student take the course as a newly returned missionary. He had been home from his mission only two or three days before he came to college as a freshman and showed up in my class—curious, diligent, thoughtful, and eager to learn. On the day we finished our unit on Buddhism, this student lingered after class. I could tell he wanted to talk, so I invited him to join me on the walk back to my office.

"I really like everything we've been learning about Buddhism," he said. "A lot of the concepts really resonate with me. But I just spent two years telling everyone who would listen that the Church of Jesus Christ of Latter-day Saints is God's one true church and inviting them to be baptized. How can the church be true—which I believe it is—if I'm also discovering truth in Buddhism, which is so different from anything I've ever heard at church or taught as a missionary?"

My student's penetrating question wasn't just about finding something in another religion that happens to harmonize with the doctrines of the restored gospel. It's easy to highlight a quotation from the Buddha because it sounds like something Jesus taught. This issue goes deeper. What does it mean that in 1831 God declared that the Church of Christ (now the Church of Jesus Christ of Latter-day Saints) was "the only true and living church upon the face of the whole earth, with which I, the Lord, am well pleased"?[1] Latter-day Saint scholar Philip Barlow suggests that "only true and living" can be read not only as a divine endorsement but also as a nineteenth-century term of endearment, the way that Joseph Smith wrote in a letter to his wife Emma that he was her "one true and living friend on Earth."[2] However we understand the phrase "only true and living church"—used only once in all of scripture—my student's question should force us to think. What does it mean for Latter-day Saints to make such strong truth claims in a world where we are a tiny minority of the global population? If truth can be found in Buddhism or Islam or secularism, why bother being a faithful Latter-day Saint? In short, how can we authentically bear testimony of being a member of "the true church" when it is evident that God is present and working through other religions too?

The 0.2 Percent

I seriously doubt Joseph Smith ever met a Buddhist. Or a Hindu, Muslim, Jain, or Zoroastrian. Some religions, such as Pentecostalism and the Bahá'í Faith, didn't even exist when he was alive. In Joseph's world, religious diversity meant Christian sectarianism. It was Methodists, Baptists, Presbyterians, Congregationalists, Campbellites, and Roman Catholics all vying for the mantle of being the true Christians, with the occasional universalist, Jew, or atheist thrown into the mix for variety. If one of the

Restoration's goals was to religiously unite the human family, it has failed spectacularly. The spiritual cacophony that sent Joseph into the grove in 1820 has only intensified and grown louder in the ensuing two centuries.

When the Restoration marked its two hundredth anniversary in 2020, members of the Church of Jesus Christ of Latter-day Saints constituted only two-tenths of one percent of the global population.[3] ("Active" church members would be less than half of that—less than one-tenth of one percent.) Because growth rates for church membership and the total world population are now roughly similar, we shouldn't expect that percentage to increase significantly anytime soon. Especially as Latter-day Saints have become more "scattered" around the world over the past half century—due to the combined forces of evangelization and migration—we have been confronted with the world's staggering religious diversity, and our pronounced minority status, in ways that previous generations of Saints living primarily in the Great Basin never did.

Our encounter with the larger world is forcing us to ask new, and sometimes challenging, questions about our place in it. What does it mean that only two-tenths of one percent of the world's population are members of "the only true and living church"? That means at least 99 percent of people around the world may have never even heard of Joseph Smith, let alone David O. McKay or Russell M. Nelson. If the Church of Jesus Christ of Latter-day Saints is true, and if God wants all his children to be members of it, shouldn't it be . . . bigger? And what about all those really good people—our neighbors, coworkers, and even our family members—who are members of other religions, or no religion at all? Can divine love, favor, and revelation really be concentrated on just two-tenths of one percent of God's children?

My head and heart both say no. The scriptures and prophets of the Church of Jesus Christ of Latter-day Saints do too.

Exclusivism and Relativism

When people assert the truth of any particular religion, their statements typically fall into one of two camps: exclusivism and relativism.

The logic of exclusivism is something like, "If A and B are qualitatively different, then if A is true, B cannot also be true." If the Notre Dame Fighting Irish are the *true* college football team, as should be obvious to any right-thinking person, then the USC Trojans cannot be, no matter the sincere beliefs of their (clearly deluded) fans. On a slightly higher plane, this is the message of monotheism: there is only one true God, so all other gods are false. The prophet Jacob taught, "the way for man is narrow . . . and the keeper of the gate is the Holy One of Israel . . . and there is none other way save it be by the gate."[4] Countless other similar statements point to the exclusivist contention that there is only one God, one heaven, one truth, and one path. Anything else is a deviation at best and damnable deception at worst. Many billions of Christians, Jews, Muslims, Hindus, Buddhists, and others have lived and died secure in their respective beliefs that their way was *the* way.

So that's the exclusivist camp: it recognizes only one legitimate path to one absolute truth. The other camp is relativism, which allows for many ways. This view was captured by Huston Smith, a well-known scholar of religion:

> It is possible to climb life's mountain from any side, but when the top is reached the trails converge. At base, in the foothills of theology, ritual, and organizational structure, the religions are distinct. Differences in culture, history, geography, and collective temperament all make for diverse starting points. Far from being deplorable, this is good; it adds richness to the totality of the human venture. . . . But beyond these differences, the same goal beckons.[5]

To relativists there are many paths up the mountain of truth; there may even be multiple peaks equally worth climbing. It doesn't matter which path you choose, so long as it leads upward and you follow it to the best of your ability. From a relativist perspective, there is no objective or absolute truth, knowledge, and morality, since those things exist only in relation to the culture or context that produced them. Therefore, "If A and B are qualitatively different, A can be true if Community X says so, and B can be true if Community Y says so." This is why cross-cultural debates about practices ranging from tipping a waiter (expected in America, insulting in China) to female genital mutilation (abhorrent in the West, traditional in many African and Arab cultures) are so difficult.[6] From a relativist standpoint, every religion is like a different facet of the same precious gem, each reflecting light in its own beautiful way.

Each camp has its attractive points. Exclusivism offers certainty, while relativism promises tolerance and goodwill. But each has its shortcomings as well. Relativism negates the real differences between religions.[7] For instance, as much as I respect and have learned from Catholicism, there is a reason (actually, many reasons) I choose to be a Latter-day Saint. Exclusivism, on the other hand, might lead me to a position of contempt or condescending pity toward Catholics or others whose faith I don't share.

I often hear Latter-day Saints decry the demerits of relativism, with good reason. But we should also be keenly aware of the dangers of religious exclusivism, knowing what it's like to be on the wrong end of it. Latter-day Saints were repeatedly the targets of very real—and at times violent—persecution in the nineteenth century, often at the hands of members of other faiths.[8] When our pioneer forebears crossed oceans and continents, they did so to find a place "where none shall come to hurt or make afraid."[9] We should therefore be deeply concerned by survey data suggesting that Utah is the second-most biased state in America against atheists and other nonreligious residents.[10] Latter-day Saints, of all people, should create communities where no one is hurt or made afraid because of what they do or don't believe.

In fact, more and more church members are increasingly uncomfortable with exclusivist language, which often has the ring of arrogance. According to one recent study, the statement "I stopped believing there was one true church" is the second most common reason people give for leaving the Church of Jesus Christ of Latter-day Saints.[11] Is there a way Latter-day Saints can authentically testify that they know the Restoration is true without sounding (or being) either naïve or intolerant? Can we chart out a faithful middle course between the excesses of both exclusivism and relativism?

Particularism

Restoration scripture says we can. In March 1831, Joseph Smith received a revelation directing how he and other elders should conduct meetings of the church. As was often the case with Joseph's revelations, inspired guidance about one thing led to another. Most of the revelation, which we have as Section 46 of the Doctrine and Covenants, focuses not on meetings but on spiritual gifts. (Perhaps there's a lesson there?) Prior to enumerating the various gifts God gives his children, the Lord states, "For all have not every gift given unto them; for there are many gifts, and to every man [and woman] is given a gift by the Spirit of God. To some is given one, and to some is given another, that all may be profited thereby." Every person on earth possesses at least one spiritual gift, but none possesses all the gifts.

Here's the key: the purpose of those gifts is to bless the lives of others—or, as the revelation says, "all these gifts come from God, for the benefit of the children of God."[12] The great range of human personalities, capacities, and talents is designed not to spark a spirit of competition or envy among God's children. Rather, we are called to discern our own gifts and share them selflessly, and we are also to recognize and appreciate the gifts of others. This is the fundamental attitude of pluralism, which accepts diversity not as a threat but rather as one of the great gifts present within the human family.

What if we were to extend the principles outlined in Section 46 to consider the ways in which God has graced not just individual women and men but also whole cultures and communities with special gifts to be shared for the benefit of all? When we do this, we begin to see how God has endowed various groups—including other religions—with particular gifts and callings that are designed to bless the world.

In 1978, the First Presidency issued an official statement regarding "God's love for all mankind." President Spencer W. Kimball and his counselors taught that "the great religious leaders of the world such as Mohammed, Confucius, and the Reformers, as well as philosophers including Socrates, Plato, and others, received a portion of God's light. Moral truths were given to them by God to enlighten whole nations and bring a higher level of understanding to individuals." While affirming that "the gospel of Jesus Christ, restored to his Church in our day," is the best way to achieve "a mortal life of happiness and a fullness of joy forever," the First Presidency testified that "God has given and will give to all people sufficient knowledge to help them on their way to eternal salvation, either in this life or in the life to come."[13]

This inspired statement refuses to peddle in either exclusivism or relativism. It does not claim that God has only sent light and knowledge to his children through the prophets of the Restoration and previous Judeo-Christian dispensations. Rather, it makes clear that God has revealed precious truths through all manner of religious leaders and philosophers on various continents and throughout history. God does this because he loves all his children, not just a select few. In this respect, the statement echoes God's own testimony, as proclaimed through the prophet Nephi: "Know ye not that there are more nations than one? Know ye not that I, the Lord your God, have created all men, and that I remember those who are upon the isles of the sea . . . and that I bring forth my word unto the children of men, yea, even upon all the nations of the earth?"[14] At the same time, however, the First Presidency's statement resists the impulse to equate or relativize disparate religious teachings. Yes, there is truth to be found among all the world's cultures and religions, but there is still something unique about the gospel of Jesus Christ as restored in this dispensation and stewarded by the Church of Jesus Christ of Latter-day Saints.

This view gives us a third camp beyond exclusivism and relativism: a position I call *particularism*. Just as individuals are blessed with particular spiritual gifts, so too are groups. These gifts are given to particular communities to bless all of God's children. The differences among the many gifts are intentional and real, and should be not only tolerated but celebrated. That means our community has distinctive gifts too. As Latter-day Saints, we need neither to retreat from our particular truth claims nor bludgeon others over the head with them. We can have confidence that we have been given talents that the Master wants us to use, not bury. At the same time, we can appreciate that he has bestowed talents on his other servants as well and has also commanded them to multiply their gifts.[15]

Throughout the scriptures, God often speaks of his work as occurring within a vineyard. For the sake of analogy, let's allow God to diversify his holdings and envision him instead as the owner of a large farm with a variety of different crops. Members of the Church of Jesus Christ of Latter-day Saints have been called to tend one particular plot of that sprawling farm, the whole of which is far too large for any one group to cultivate. Other communities—different religions and cultures—have in turn been given stewardship over other plots. All the different sections of the farm are interdependent; if one suffers from blight or lack of tending, it can negatively affect the surrounding plots. On the other hand, when one section yields a bounteous harvest, it can be shared with all. We labor with all our might, mind, and strength in our particular corner of the farm, knowing that the crops we raise are absolutely essential. At the same time, we recognize that our fellow laborers are doing equally good and valuable work tending to their respective crops.

There are some crops—faith, hope, love, prayer, service, family, care for the poor, the sanctity of life, religious freedom—that are planted in the commons at the center of the farm, open to anyone to both nurture and harvest. But the cultivation of many other particular crops seems to have been divvied out to different groups—not to hoard but to steward and then share. From my perspective, evangelical Christians have expertly cultivated the grace section; Buddhists have cultivated meditation; Jains have cultivated nonviolence; and so forth. Secular communities such as government and science also have their important stewardships. Of course, most gifts and stewardships can't be reduced to one word or phrase, and some crops may be tended in multiple plots. But the beauty of this diversified arrangement is found in the reality that some groups simply do some things better than others. A group's spiritual gifts may be best indicated by what they do well, what they feel a sense of calling or vocation toward, where they put their greatest energies, and what gives them the greatest joy and sense of connection to both God and their fellow humans.

So what "crops" have Latter-day Saints been uniquely assigned to cultivate, protect from harm, harvest, and distribute to all? I suggest there are five of them:[16]

1. Restoration scripture (the Book of Mormon, Doctrine and Covenants, and Pearl of Great Price)

2. Modern prophets and apostles beginning with Joseph Smith
3. Priesthood, as exercised by the Aaronic and Melchizedek orders and by all endowed women and men in the temple
4. The "new and everlasting covenant," consisting of the covenants and ordinances that culminate in the ceremonies of the temple
5. A distinctive view of God's plan of salvation, based on the human potential to become like God and on family-based exaltation

Other religions have holy books, inspired leaders, spiritual power, and beautiful rituals. Other people love their families, have great ideas, and foster effective social arrangements. But no other community has been given stewardship over these *particular* five things—each of which, as we can testify, brings almost unspeakable light, power, love, truth, and goodness into people's lives and into the world. As partakers and proclaimers of the Restoration, it is Latter-day Saints' special calling to tend to and distribute these five crops. And when we do, we can confidently testify that the Church of Jesus Christ of Latter-day Saints is true to the mission and stewardship that God has given it.

The Body of Christ

Having exhausted the agricultural metaphor, let me turn to an anatomical one, compliments of the apostle Paul. Typically we think of the body of Christ as the church; indeed, that was Paul's original usage and intent. But let's consider the body of Christ to be all those bodies whom Christ loves and redeems—namely, the whole family of God. Taking it further, let's consider the parts of that greater body to be not individuals but groups—cultures, peoples, even religions. Paul's metaphor then takes on different meaning and sharpens our understanding of particularism:

> Indeed, the body does not consist of one member but of many. . . . If the whole body were an eye, where would the hearing be? If the whole body were hearing, where would the sense of smell be? But as it is, God arranged the members of the body, and each one of them, as he chose. . . . The eye cannot say to the hand, "I have no need of you," nor again the head to the feet, "I have no need of you." On the contrary, the members of the body that seem to be weaker are indispensable.[17]

Healthy functioning of the body depends on an elegant and efficient division of specialized labor within an interdependent system. That is to say, each part has its own separate role to play within the whole. No matter how distinctive and essential each of those parts is, however, none can survive without being connected to and integrated with all the others. Body parts can't afford to be exclusivist or relativist—no single part has a fundamentally "true" function while the others are all false, nor can the parts pretend that they all do essentially the same thing. The eye is "true" when the eye does what the eye was designed to do. The eye would be false, however, if it were to quit functioning, pretend to be something else, try to exist on its own, or suppose that it is superior to all the other parts because they don't do what it does. Just because one part of the body plays an essential function does not mean that it plays the *only* important or necessary function. The heart is absolutely unique and essential in providing blood and vital oxygen to the whole body. But try separating the heart from the nervous system, lungs, arteries, veins, and even tiny capillaries, and see how far it goes. The corollary is also true: the heart must understand that even though it is not the only essential member, if it does not offer its gifts "whole-heartedly" to the rest of the parts, the body will not be healthy. Our bodies operate on the principle of particularism.

You can think about the Church of Jesus Christ of Latter-day Saints as whatever part of the body you want—the heart, the brain, the lungs, maybe the liver (thank you, Word of Wisdom). The important point is that our church is not the whole body—remember, it constitutes only two-tenths of a percent of its total mass. That's not nothing, but there are a lot of things that two-tenths of a percent simply cannot do. Take, for instance, the COVID-19 global pandemic. All the faith, prayers, fasting, service, and dollars of the Church of Jesus Christ of Latter-day Saints, however significant, were not enough on their own to stop the virus or alleviate all the suffering it caused, even in Utah where the church is most concentrated. In relation to the massive needs of the global body, our positive impact on public health, humanitarian relief, and welfare assistance during the pandemic was real but minuscule. So while we aim to relieve all kinds of suffering within the body, we cannot forget our unique calling, which is to take care of those things that make us distinctive. We have been called to perform essential functions that no other part of the body does, and in doing so we contribute to the health of the whole body.

Gifts, Not Entitlements

Gifts are subject to misuse when we mistake them for entitlements. It's important to remember that gifts are neither earned nor deserved but are rather bestowals of grace from the Giver of all good things and are intended for the benefit of all. Yet pride always lurks in the background, sometimes nearer than we want to admit. To help keep us humble, the Lord reminds us that even the special gifts he has given to and through the Restoration are not meant as tokens of his exclusive favor.

Yes, Restoration scripture is irreplaceable. But we have no monopoly on the loquaciousness of God, whose children all around the world will produce (or perhaps have already produced) the scriptures containing the words he has spoken to them.[18] We have a particular stewardship over that unmatched second witness of Christ, the Book of Mormon, but that also comes with a solemn responsibility to live by its teachings.[19]

Yes, God has set apart prophets and apostles for distinctive, foundational roles within the body of Christ, and yes, church members have covenanted to sustain them and hearken to their words. They uniquely hold the keys of the priesthood. But as the First Presidency taught, God has also called others around the world and throughout history to speak his words and do his will. Our community does not have a corner on holy men and women.[20]

Yes, the priesthood is the power and authority of God delegated to his children on earth. It is an incomparable blessing. But that priesthood can never be self-serving and "cannot be controlled nor handled only upon the principles of righteousness." Whether given through the Aaronic, Melchizedek, or temple orders, the priesthood only has any effect when practiced with the Christlike qualities of persuasion, longsuffering, gentleness, meekness, kindness, pure knowledge, and most of all love. If as individuals or as a church we ever invoke the priesthood "to cover our sins, or to gratify our pride," then we forfeit the authority to act in God's name.[21]

Yes, our church has been given authority to provide the necessary ordinances to prepare God's children for salvation and exaltation through the new and everlasting covenant. But God has given the Restoration the magnificent and daunting assignment of performing temple ordinances for *all* God's family, living and dead. That means that eventually every person will be baptized, every person will be endowed, every person will be sealed. The ordinances and their associated covenants are therefore like the vital organs in every human body—absolutely essential, absolutely special, and absolutely universal.

Yes, we have privileged access to revealed knowledge about who we really are—actual children of a divine Mother and Father whose entire work and glory is for us to become like they are. And yes, we find great comfort in knowing that exaltation is a family affair, that the same loving relationships that enrich life here will do so in the eternities. But the kingdom of God can't be reduced to a Norman Rockwell portrait of Thanksgiving dinner. The nuclear family can become an idol that blinds and alienates as much as it enlightens and binds. Our Heavenly Parents' plan of salvation was never focused on preserving *your* family so much as reconciling and exalting *theirs*.

God's grand aim—"the restoration of his people"—is too much for two-tenths of one percent of his family to accomplish on our own.[22] Thankfully, our Parents have recruited all their children to work on the farm, some near and others distant from our immediate view. That they have also assigned others to work their respective plots, however, does not minimize the fact that they have called me and you to do this particular work, in this particular place, at this particular time, among this particular (and peculiar) people. The work assigned to the stewardship of the Church of Jesus Christ of Latter-day Saints is essential, it is living, and it is true. The Lord invites us to "lay hold upon every good thing" cultivated in every part of the garden.[23] But God also needs us to put our whole hearts into working this particular patch, so that all our sisters and brothers can eat of its truly good and irreplaceable fruits.

NOTES

1. Doctrine and Covenants 1:30.
2. "Letter to Emma Smith, 13 October 1832," p. [2], The Joseph Smith Papers, accessed 7 August 2020, https://www.josephsmithpapers.org/paper-summary/letter-to-emma-smith-13-october-1832/2. See Philip Barlow, "The Only True and Living Church?," 12 April 2020, https://faithmatters.org/the-only-true-and-living-church/.
3. I divided the church membership of approximately 16,500,000 by the total world population of approximately 7,800,000,000.
4. 2 Nephi 9:41. See also Matthew 7:13–14.
5. Huston Smith, *The World's Religions* (New York: HarperOne, 1991), 73.
6. Relativism is famously difficult to define. See "Relativism," Stanford Encyclopedia of Philosophy, https://plato.stanford.edu/entries/relativism/; or, for a more accessible approach, "Relativism," https://philosophyterms.com/relativism/, both accessed 17 July 2020.
7. This is the basic premise of my favorite primer on comparative religions—Stephen Prothero, *God Is Not One: The Eight Rival Religions that Run the World—and Why Their Differences Matter* (San Francisco: HarperOne, 2010).
8. See Patrick Q. Mason, *The Mormon Menace: Violence and Anti-Mormonism in the Postbellum South* (New York: Oxford University Press, 2011).
9. "Come, Come Ye Saints," *Hymns* (Salt Lake City: The Church of Jesus Christ of Latter-day Saints, 1985), #30.
10. Peggy Fletcher Stack, "Utah Is the Second Most Biased State against Nonreligious Residents, Survey Says," *Salt Lake Tribune*, 6 May 2020.
11. Jana Riess, *The Next Mormons: How Millennials Are Changing the LDS Church* (New York: Oxford University Press, 2019), 224.
12. Doctrine and Covenants 46, quotes from verses 11–12, 26. See also 1 Corinthians 12:4–11; Moroni 10:8–18.
13. "Statement of the First Presidency Regarding God's Love for All Mankind," quoted in Miranda Wilcox and John D. Young, eds., *Standing Apart: Mormon Historical Consciousness and the Concept of Apostasy* (New York: Oxford University Press, 2014), 343.
14. 2 Nephi 29:7.
15. See Matthew 25:14–30.
16. This list echoes but is not exactly the same as the "purpose of the

Church" as outlined in the *General Handbook: Serving in The Church of Jesus Christ of Latter-day Saints* (Salt Lake City: The Church of Jesus Christ of Later-day Saints, 2020), 1.3.

17. 1 Corinthians 12:14–22 (NRSV).

18. See 2 Nephi 29:12.

19. See Doctrine and Covenants 84:57.

20. Doctrine and Covenants 49:8; see 1 Corinthians 12:22–29; Ephesians 2:20; Doctrine and Covenants 21:4–5.

21. Doctrine and Covenants 121:36–37, 41–42.

22. 2 Nephi 30:8.

23. Moroni 7:19.

CHAPTER FIVE

Excess Baggage

My first job as a tenure-track professor was teaching United States history at the American University in Cairo. In a city that is more than a thousand years old and a civilization that began more than five thousand years ago, it was a little daunting teaching the history of a nation that hasn't yet celebrated its 250th birthday. As one of my Egyptian students aptly quipped, "America doesn't have history—it's all just current events."

I feel that way whenever I talk about the Restoration with my colleagues who study Judaism, Buddhism, and Hinduism—religions that are literally thousands of years old. To them, even two-thousand-year-old Christianity is "new," and Islam is practically a baby with only fourteen centuries of history under its belt. A religion that's not even two hundred years old? It's all just current events.

Rather than feeling insecure about the newness of the Restoration, I'm energized knowing that the Restoration is here to stay, and that most of its history lies ahead. It's pretty exciting to know that you're actively shaping the development of a religion that's still new in terms of world history.

But before we look to the future, as we will in the next chapter, it's important to take stock of where we are and where we've been. As James Baldwin wrote, "the past is all that makes the present coherent."¹ I don't want to recount the details of our collective history, which can be found in any number of other excellent books.² Instead, I want to consider how the Restoration's first two centuries set the trajectory we find ourselves on now. There are some precious aspects of that history that we should cling to with all our strength—heroic and faith-filled stories we should never tire of telling and retelling. But along the way we've also picked up some extra cargo. With the benefit of hindsight, and always with generosity and charity toward those who have come before, we're in a position now to determine which elements of the historical and cultural baggage we have gathered on our journey we want to keep and which ones we may want to leave by the wayside as the Restoration moves forward.

The Past Is a Foreign Country

Whenever students take one of my history classes, I want them to learn two basic principles. First, history is the study of change over time—so get comfortable with the fact that the way things are now is not the way they have always been nor will be. Second, as the novelist L. P. Hartley wrote, "the past is a foreign country: they do things differently there."[3]

Even in the Restoration's relatively short two-century history, there has been a tremendous amount of change. While we have much in common with our pioneer forebears, many aspects of the church and culture they built in the Restoration's first century would seem quite foreign to us today.

For instance, were we to hop in a time machine and set the dial for 1870, fifty years after Joseph Smith's First Vision, we might be surprised by what we find.[4] Church leaders in territorial Utah often simultaneously held ecclesiastical and political office, with little or no separation of church and state. Polygamy was the stated ideal, with church members strongly encouraged to practice plural marriage to shore up their inheritance in heaven. Sacrament meeting attendance was spotty at best, the Word of Wisdom wasn't honored in a way we would recognize, and being a faithful Latter-day Saint didn't include regular temple attendance or family history work. There were no Primary or Young Women's or Young Men's organizations; the Relief Society was only just being reorganized after a hiatus of over two decades. If a woman was sick, she would be just as likely to call the sisters as the elders to give her a blessing of healing.

A bit bewildered, we might return to our time machine and set the controls for a half century later. We would breathe a sigh of relief upon stepping out in 1920, when the church would start to look familiar. Even so, many things would be quite different.

The Book of Mormon? Surprisingly underutilized in church publications and teachings until the 1980s, when President Ezra Taft Benson challenged all church members to make the book the "keystone" of their testimonies.[5]

Missionary work? Always important, but only a tiny fraction of church members went on missions until after World War II, when President David O. McKay proclaimed "every member a missionary."[6]

Correlation? The church's various auxiliaries and priesthood quorums all became consolidated under the direction of the Twelve Apostles and local Melchizedek Priesthood leadership only beginning in the 1960s. The *Ensign*, *New Era*, *Friend*, and *Liahona* all date to the 1970s. The current "block" schedule of Sunday meetings only began in 1980.

Temples? The church had six operating temples in 1924 when Russell M. Nelson was born. By 2018, when he was set apart as president of the church, 159 temples were in operation, with thirty-five more announced in the ensuing two years. Ninety-six percent of current operating temples were dedicated during President Nelson's lifetime, most of those since his ordination as an apostle in 1984.[7]

Church growth? The Church of Jesus Christ of Latter-day Saints didn't hit the one-million-member mark until 1947, over a century after its founding. It then took sixteen years to reach two million members (in 1963), and another eight years to get to three (in 1971). Though growth has slowed down over the past decade, for the past half century the church has, on average, been adding a million new members about every four years.

A global church? In 1955, 92 percent of Latter-day Saints lived in the United States; four decades later, in 1996, the church announced that for the first time the majority of its members lived outside the U.S.

In short, most recognizable features of contemporary Latter-day Saint religious life date not to the Restoration's first century but its second. And as President Nelson has made clear, we should expect more change in the future. Change means growth and development, but it also may entail leaving behind certain things. For us to move forward into the Restoration's third century, it's important for us to assess whether there are any teachings, practices, or habits from its first two centuries that are weighing us down and will hinder our progress.

Baggage

Two cardinal rules of airports: don't grab anyone else's baggage, and don't accept items from strangers. And if you try to travel with excess baggage, it will cost you.

The Restoration does not exist independently from culture, so it's inevitable and even good that the Restoration takes on many aspects of the society in which it finds itself. In fact, the only way the gospel can find its way into people's hearts is if they find it relevant to their everyday lives. One of the foundational doctrines of Christianity is the incarnation—namely, that God took on flesh, and by doing so entered into human life and culture. The trick, of course, is how to take on flesh without becoming fleshy, how to be in the world but not of it, how to engage culture without becoming captive to it.

Preached and practiced by humans, the Restoration has not been immune to the harmful effects of cultural captivity. Choose your own metaphor: barnacles on the ship, clutter in the closet, monkeys on our back, extra weight in the backpack. In the Lord's definition, the nature of modern-day idolatry is that "every man walketh in his own way, and after the image of his own god, whose image is in the likeness of the world."[8] At various points over the past two centuries, and often as a result of good or at least understandable intentions, the Restoration has in some respects taken on "the likeness of the world" by adopting certain aspects of the surrounding culture—principally American culture. Unfortunately, some of this unnecessary baggage has compromised our ability as a people to fully accomplish the Restoration's purposes; it has cost us. If we want to receive the full message that God is revealing at the top of Sinai, then we need to tear down the graven images we have forged down below in the likeness of some of the modern world's false gods: racism, patriarchy, nationalism, cultural colonialism, inequality, and fundamentalism.

Racism. One of Satan's great deceptions is to turn God-given diversity into enmity. Prejudice is not a new phenomenon; even some Nephite prophets struggled with it.[9] But it has only been in the past few centuries that humans have truly perfected the wicked art of racism, producing various evils from slavery to segregation to apartheid to the Holocaust.[10]

Racism in any form is sin. As President Nelson affirmed in the wake of the worldwide protests for racial equality in the summer of 2020, "The Creator of us all calls on each of us to abandon attitudes of prejudice against any group of God's children. Any of us who has prejudice toward another race needs to repent!"[11]

Latter-day Saints do not have a perfect record when it comes to dealing with racial difference. God's standard was made clear at the Restoration's outset: "he inviteth them all to come unto him and partake of his goodness; and he denieth none that come unto him, black and white, bond and free, male and female; and he remembereth the heathen; and all are alike unto God, both Jew and Gentile."[12] But on this score the Saints have too often hearkened to the voices of white Euro-American culture rather than the voice of the Lord.[13] It's not just the 126-year ban preventing people of African descent from being ordained to the priesthood or participating in temple ordinances.[14] It was pioneers participating in the Indian slave trade and violently dispossessing Native Americans of their lands.[15] It was Latter-day Saint legislators writing laws formalizing racialized "servitude" and banning interracial marriage.[16] It is the ongoing racism evident in the modern church that provoked two prophets, Gordon B. Hinckley and Russell M. Nelson, to call the Saints to repentance.[17]

How can we effectively fulfill our duty to take the restored gospel of Jesus Christ to all the world—the majority of which is not white—if the Restoration carries any whiff of white racism? Even more than four decades after President Spencer W. Kimball's 1978 revelation rescinding the priesthood-temple ban, the Restoration still suffers reputational damage for its history of racial prejudice. The sins of the fathers continue to be visited upon the children. White nationalism still rears its ugly head among some of our people. Racism in any form is baggage we should have unloaded long ago. We need the courage to lovingly reverse race-based prejudice wherever we find it—even, or especially, among our brothers and sisters in the church. We need acknowledgment, repentance, repair, and reconciliation.

Patriarchy. Latter-day Saints didn't invent patriarchy, or male domination; there is probably no form of social hierarchy more ancient, pervasive, or entrenched. It was therefore probably inevitable that members of the church would adopt many ideas about men and women from their surrounding culture and then load those ideas into the Restoration as if they were there all along. Our theology recognizes the common-sense observation that there are fundamental biological differences between men and women, and that some kind of sexual distinction persists in the eternities since we have both a Heavenly Mother and Heavenly Father. Yet Restoration scripture has surprisingly little by way of prescriptive statements about particular social roles that all men or women are supposed to play as men or women.

Plural marriage worsened patriarchy among the Saints. It magnified existing Euro-American cultural norms regarding male leadership and female subservience in the home, the church, and society. Latter-day Saint patriarchy has taken many forms but was perhaps most succinctly articulated by Brigham Young when he taught, "God never in any age of the world endowed woman with knowledge above the man."[18] Another nineteenth-century apologist for polygamy, Benjamin F. Johnson, rhetorically asked, "Where upon the 'pages of inspiration,' is there one evidence that woman was designed to fill a sphere equal with man?"[19] Our history is unfortunately full of other, equally infuriating examples.

There are many complex and fair questions to be asked about how sex and gender should be understood in light of the Restoration, but Brother Johnson's query is not among them. No matter how we grapple with the subject, the Restoration should compel us to proceed from the simple fundamental truth expressed clearly in the pages of inspiration: "male and female . . . are alike unto God."[20] The demeaning of women in many cultures and throughout history has been a recurrent sign of—and contributor to—spiritual darkness.[21]

Personally, I don't have a great answer to some of our own community's most vexing questions on this score, including the issue of women's ordination. I lean on my fellow Saints, especially sisters, for their wisdom.[22] What I do know is that if our conversations, practices, or policies begin from any premise other than women's and men's fundamental "alikeness" in the sight of God, we are more often influenced by patriarchal cultural baggage than we are by the restored gospel of Jesus Christ. We can start unloading our baggage by recognizing and renouncing any notion of male chauvinism that has infected the Restoration past or present.

Nationalism. Here's a thought experiment I do with my students. Answer honestly:

If necessary, are you willing to die for your country?
If necessary, are you willing to die for your religion?
If necessary, are you willing to kill for your country?
If necessary, are you willing to kill for your religion?

I'm guessing you probably answered yes to the first and second questions, hesitated but said yes to the third, and felt at least a minor sense of revulsion at the fourth. It seems good and honorable to be willing to die for the things we love, especially on behalf of other people. After all, as Jesus taught (and exemplified), "No one has greater love than this, to lay down one's life for one's friends."[23] And most people recognize that if their nation goes to war, they may be called upon to not only die but also kill for their country.

But to kill for your religion? That sounds more like the Crusades or ISIS than the Restoration.

The author of this thought experiment, the Christian theologian William Cavanaugh, suggests that most people's willingness to kill for their country but not for their religion reveals the way the nation-state has set itself up as an absolute authority that functionally operates as a rival, if not a replacement, for God in modern times. As Cavanaugh concludes, "at least among American

Christians, the nation-state—[Thomas] Hobbes's 'mortal god'—is subject to far more absolutist fervor than religion."[24] By this measure, at least, the nation-state is an idol—or, in President Spencer W. Kimball's words, a "false god."[25]

To be clear, I'm not suggesting you should be willing to kill for the Restoration. Quite the contrary. What I am proposing is that Latter-day Saints might think harder than we typically do about what claim the nation-state has on our loyalties and affections. Are we Americans (or Mexicans, or Filipinos) first, or citizens of the kingdom of God? Is it possible to be "subject to" secular governmental authorities without uncritically worshiping at Caesar's altar?[26] The Restoration does not call us to withdraw from political society, but neither does it consider the nation holy. National identities dissolve in the kingdom of God, a fact both aspired to and largely achieved in our temples. As Paul wrote to first-century believers, "You are no longer foreigners and noncitizens, but you are fellow citizens with the saints and household of God."[27] Insofar as we ever elevate our national identity over our common identity as children of God, we have some bags to unpack. As M. Russell Ballard, president of the Quorum of the Twelve Apostles, asserted, "We need to embrace God's children compassionately and eliminate any prejudice, including racism, sexism, and nationalism."[28]

This principle extends to the political partisanship that fractures communities and poisons relationships—especially on social media but also in wards and stakes. Church leaders have repeatedly expressed political neutrality and the importance of the church not being too closely affiliated with any particular political party.[29] The kingdom of God doesn't map onto party platforms; when Jesus returns, it won't be to a party convention. Political engagement is good, but if our partisanship compromises our Christianity, we need to reconsider which bags we're carrying and for whom.

Cultural colonialism. One of my most memorable experiences from graduate school came in a seminar taught by an accomplished anthropologist. As the professor recounted various examples of violence wrought on native populations around the world at the hands of Christian evangelists, she started pounding on her desk and exclaimed, "*I hate missionaries!*" She didn't know that I had returned from my mission only a few years before, but my classmates did, so every eye turned toward me. A spirited exchange ensued.

Fortunately, the Church of Jesus Christ of Latter-day Saints is young and small enough not to have been implicated in the worst abuses of Christian colonialism and imperialism from the fifteenth through nineteenth centuries. Unfortunately, we took many of our cues about global evangelization from the churches that Jesus commanded Joseph Smith not to join. Too many of our missionaries have taken upon themselves the proverbial "white man's burden" to not only save but also "civilize," which invariably means to Americanize. The messengers have too often confused the packaging for the package. In the name of consistency and unity, as a church we have taken a highly cautious approach to both indigenization (local control of church institutions) and enculturation (the absorption of local customs, styles, and norms).[30] If something isn't considered sacred in Utah culture (say, drumming), we've typically said it can't be sacred anywhere else (say, Africa).

Christianity and Islam became the world's two most prominent religions because over the centuries they learned to adapt themselves to diverse cultures and empower local people while retaining a core identity. For the Restoration to be relevant and influential throughout the entire world, we will need to determine what are non-negotiables in terms of faith and practice, and what forms of diversity actually enhance our ability to worship God and serve one another in disparate local contexts. We can start with the simple things, like dress and grooming standards (do all

Latter-day Saint men have to look like they work for IBM in the 1950s?), worship music (where our emphasis on "reverence" can make even hymns of praise sound like dirges), and sacred art (Jesus was *not* Scandinavian!). Then we can tackle the slightly tougher questions, like which local beverages are in or out in terms of the Word of Wisdom, before we get to the really tricky issues, like bridewealth in many African cultures.[31]

Crucially, Salt Lake mustn't always dictate the terms of the conversation, let alone make all the decisions. Faithful Saints on the ground need to be our guides. Other Christian churches in the West are being renewed by the spirituality and vitality of their sisters and brothers in the global South—those who for many centuries were the objects of Euro-American missionary work. If our church's spiritual economy has heavily favored American cultural exports over imports in the past, the Restoration's third century may be the time to rebalance the ledger.

Inequality of wealth. Sometimes the baggage we accumulate is less about picking up bad habits than letting go of good ones. One of the most consistent targets of divine condemnation throughout Restoration scripture is inequality—especially inequality of wealth. The Restoration has never ennobled poverty, but it does privilege the needs and wants of the poor and fiercely denounces anyone who acts with callous disregard toward them. Jesus was not a capitalist; he cared nothing about the accumulation of material wealth. The same held true for his most immediate disciples in both Jerusalem and the promised land. The Bible and Book of Mormon unitedly attest that the people who most directly experienced the resurrected Lord created a new type of community in which "they had all things common among them; therefore there were not rich and poor."[32] Other Zion societies have similarly organized their economic life so that "there was no poor among them"—not by way of building enclosed communities that kept the poor out, but rather "in their prosperous circumstances, they did not send away any who were naked, or that were hungry." Why give away their hard-earned money? Because "they did not set their hearts upon riches; therefore they were liberal to all."[33]

It may be that free market capitalism is the least bad economy that humans can devise and implement in a telestial world. We can point to the real social goods that capitalism has enabled; the global standard of living has increased dramatically over the past century. At the same time, one of the byproducts of modern capitalism has been the growth of inequality. For instance, in the United States, the bottom half of households own less than 2 percent of the nation's wealth, whereas the top 10 percent own almost three-quarters.[34] Christians and other people of goodwill can disagree about what degree of inequality is palatable and how best to remedy it, but Restoration scriptures insist that we keep the problem squarely in our view.

The early Saints strove to create economic arrangements that would mitigate inequality and provide generously for all. In 1875, the church's First Presidency and Quorum of the Twelve Apostles denounced the American capitalist system because it created "the wonderful growth of wealth in the hands of a comparatively few individuals." Without dismissing the virtues of a market-based economy, the apostles called the church and its members to create an alternative economic system based on the principle of cooperation, not competition.[35]

However, a subtle shift occurred in the church over the next two generations, when personal wealth came to be seen as the rightful reward for individual initiative and hard work. The Saints had once viewed prosperity through a communitarian lens—acquired wealth was a gift from God for the good of all. But after the pioneer generation passed away, they came to regard wealth in much the same terms as the rest of American culture, as a means to maximize the interests of the private individual or corporation.[36] Simply put, we picked up America's allergy to talking about inequality and began to skim over scriptural mandates that had once been central to the Restoration. Despite the Lord's consistent and stern warnings, we have largely been seduced by the gods of affluence and ease. Many of us orient our lives around this pursuit. At times we have even verged dangerously close to embracing a Latter-day Saint version of the "prosperity gospel," the operating assumptions of which are that God wants us to be rich and comfortable, and that wealth is a sign of his favor. That is not the gospel Jesus preached.

To be sure, the Saints remain a generous people, committed to private acts of charity and humanitarianism. But the Restoration's initial deposit of faith—meaning the body of revealed truth given in scripture and the apostolic tradition—emphasized consecration, not capital. The Restoration's economic worldview should be shaped more by Joseph Smith than Adam Smith. Picking up the cultural baggage of inequality has led us to forget some of what we once knew.

Fundamentalism. From 1910 to 1915, a group of Protestant scholars and writers published a series of ninety essays in twelve paperback volumes collectively called *The Fundamentals*. The essays defended the inerrancy of the Bible, established rigorous anti-modernist positions on various theological questions, and critiqued all manner of dangerous "isms," including Darwinism, spiritualism, Catholicism, and Mormonism. The book series gave rise to the term "fundamentalism."[37]

Latter-day Saints didn't create fundamentalism; we were actually targeted as enemies by the original fundamentalists. But in the mid-twentieth century, we imported fundamentalistic thinking into our church and culture. I'm not referring to "Mormon fundamentalists," who maintain plural marriage and other distinctive nineteenth-century doctrines and practices. Rather, I mean that in the first half of the twentieth century, a new generation of church leaders and members adopted some of the fundamentalists' strategies. They began to emphasize Mormonism's unique and exclusive authority, to talk less about theology and more about adhering to a strict moral code, and to distrust the academic and intellectual work that an earlier generation had pursued.[38] They often took novel doctrinaire positions and expressed them as being timeless. Virtually every fundamentalistic position taken in our church in the twentieth century, whether it be on biological evolution, gender roles, the historicity of scripture, or the preeminence of the King James Version, was adapted from views first worked out by conservative Protestants and then translated into a Latter-day Saint dialect.

Fundamentalist Protestants took some important stands that we should celebrate and share, particularly around the divinity of Jesus and the reality of his bodily resurrection. But isn't it a bit strange that for several decades we took many of our theological cues from the group most doggedly opposed to Restoration theology? In a classic case of what the scholar René Girard called "mimetic rivalry," we began to imitate our rivals, adopting their own tools, techniques, and blueprints in order to build our own supposedly impregnable fortress church.[39]

Introducing too much rigidity into a system can actually increase rather than decrease its risk of failure when subjected to extreme pressure. That is why skyscrapers are designed to sway a few inches in the wind—it's an unsettling feeling when you're on the top floors, but it's far preferable to having the building collapse underneath you. The same thing is true of yoga, in which locking your knees while stretching too far can lead to injury. For two or three generations, we pursued a strategy of trying to eliminate movement and flexibility within our religious system. We tried to lock down every practice and point of doctrine, no matter how great or small. This is most obvious in various cultural practices that we confused for doctrine. For a while, having "the priesthood" preside at meetings meant that women could not give closing talks or prayers. Overly strict interpretations of the Word of Wisdom meant that drinking a Diet Coke could mark you as a pariah. And woe be to the man who wore a blue shirt or a woman who wore pants to church!

The irony is that this fundamentalistic intolerance for ambiguity, complexity, and difference eventually made us *less* resilient to various stressors, not more.[40] An entire cottage industry has arisen in recent years to tear down this too-rigid system; they've found it embarrassingly easy to point out and exploit its structural flaws. Fortunately, we have also begun the overdue work of redesigning the system to correct for our earlier excesses. Building upon Christ as our cornerstone, apostles and prophets as our foundation, and the Book of Mormon as our keystone still allows us great latitude for tailoring the design and function of the church to the needs of both its members and the broader world.

And that's the reality for all of these pieces of baggage, these heavy steamer trunks handed down from earlier generations. The good news is that we can streamline for a new century with confidence, knowing that the Restoration's foundations are strong and its basic structures are sound. The ongoing Restoration is a constantly new creation, alive and breathing and developing. It's informed by, but not captive to, the past. By knowing where we've been and taking accountability for our many successes and occasional missteps, we can better anticipate where we're going. By lightening our load of unwanted, unneeded, and costly excess baggage, we will be less encumbered as we stride confidently into the future and make the Restoration's third century a worthy successor to its first two.

NOTES

1. James Baldwin, *Notes of a Native Son* (Boston: Beacon Press, 1955/2012), 6.

2. The best one-volume history of the Latter-day Saints is Matthew Bowman, *The Mormon People: The Making of an American Faith* (New York: Random House, 2012). I'm also deeply impressed with the church's ongoing narrative history, *Saints: The Story of the Church of Jesus Christ in the Latter Days*, available online at https://history.churchofjesuschrist.org/saints.

3. L. P. Hartley, *The Go-Between* (New York: New York Review Books Classics, 2002), 17.

4. The classic articulation of this thought experiment is Jan Shipps, *Mormonism: The Story of a New Religious Tradition* (Urbana: University of Illinois Press, 1985), 109–111.

5. See Noel B. Reynolds, "The Coming Forth of the Book of Mormon in the Twentieth Century," *BYU Studies Quarterly* 38:2 (1999): 6–47.

6. See Gregory A. Prince and Wm. Robert Wright, *David O. McKay and the Rise of Modern Mormonism* (Salt Lake City: University of Utah Press, 2005), chap. 10.

7. David A. Bednar, "Let This House Be Built unto My Name," April 2020 General Conference, https://www.churchofjesuschrist.org/study/general-conference/2020/04/44bednar?lang=eng.

8. Doctrine and Covenants 1:16.

9. See Jacob 3:5–10; Enos 1:11–20.

10. See George M. Fredrickson, *Racism: A Short History* (Princeton, NJ: Princeton University Press, 2002).

11. "President Nelson Shares Social Post about Racism and Calls for Respect for Human Dignity," Newsroom, 1 June 2020, https://newsroom.churchofjesuschrist.org/article/president-nelson-shares-social-post-encouraging-understanding-and-civility, accessed 16 July 2020.

12. 2 Nephi 26:33.

13. See Joanna Brooks, *Mormonism and White Supremacy: American Religion and the Problem of Racial Innocence* (New York: Oxford University Press, 2020).

14. The best account of the origins of the priesthood-temple ban is W. Paul Reeve, *Religion of a Different Color: Race and the Mormon Struggle for Whiteness* (New York: Oxford University Press, 2015), especially chapters 4–5. For the church's acknowledgment of this history, see the Gospel Topics essay

"Race and the Priesthood," https://www.churchofjesuschrist.org/study/manual/gospel-topics/race-and-the-priesthood?lang=eng.

15. Brian Q. Cannon, "'To Buy Up the Lamanite Children as Fast as They Could': Indentured Servitude and Its Legacy in Mormon Society," *Journal of Mormon History* 44:2 (April 2018): 1–35. See also the church's essay on "Indian Slavery and Indentured Servitude," at https://www.churchofjesuschrist.org/study/history/topics/indian-slavery-and-indentured-servitude?lang=eng.

16. Patrick Q. Mason, "The Prohibition of Interracial Marriage in Utah, 1888–1963," *Utah Historical Quarterly* 76:2 (Spring 2008): 108–31.

17. Gordon B. Hinckley, "The Need for Greater Kindness," April 2006 General Conference, https://www.churchofjesuschrist.org/study/general-conference/2006/04/the-need-for-greater-kindness?lang=eng.

18. Juanita Brooks, ed., *Not by Bread Alone: The Journal of Martha Spence Heywood, 1850–1856* (Salt Lake City: Utah State Historical Society, 1978), 122.

19. Quoted in B. Carmon Hardy, "Lords of Creation: Polygamy, the Abrahamic Household, and Mormon Patriarchy," *Journal of Mormon History* 20:1 (Spring 1994): 132.

20. 2 Nephi 26:33.

21. See Jean B. Bingham, "United in Accomplishing God's Work," April 2020 General Conference.

22. For some excellent recent treatments, see Neylan McBaine, *Women at Church: Magnifying LDS Women's Local Impact* (Draper, UT: Greg Kofford Books, 2014); Joanna Brooks, Rachel Hunt Steenblik, and Hannah Wheelwright, eds., *Mormon Feminism: Essential Writings* (New York: Oxford University Press, 2016); Carol Lynn Pearson, *The Ghost of Eternal Polygamy: Haunting the Hearts and Heaven of Mormon Women and Men* (Walnut Creek, CA: Pivot Point Books, 2016); Hollie Rhees Fluhman and Camille Fronk Olson, eds., *A Place to Belong: Reflections from Modern Latter-day Saint Women* (Salt Lake City: Deseret Book Co., 2019); Melissa Inouye, *Crossings: A Bald Asian American Latter-day Saint Woman Scholar's Ventures through Life, Death, Cancer, and Motherhood* (Provo and Salt Lake City: Neal A. Maxwell Institute for Religious Scholarship and Deseret Book Co., 2019); Barbara Morgan Gardner, *The Priesthood Power of Women: In the Temple, Church, and Home* (Salt Lake City: Deseret Book Co., 2019).

23. John 15:13 (NRSV).

24. William T. Cavanaugh, *The Myth of Religious Violence* (New York: Oxford University Press, 2009), 56.

25. Spencer W. Kimball, "The False Gods We Worship," *Ensign* (June 1976).

26. Articles of Faith 1:12.

27. Ephesians 2:19, in Thomas A. Wayment, *The New Testament: A Translation for Latter-day Saints: A Study Bible* (Provo and Salt Lake City: Religious Studies Center and Deseret Book Co., 2019).

28. M. Russell Ballard, "The Trek Continues!" October 2017 General Conference.

29. See Dan Harrie, "GOP Dominance Troubles Church," *Salt Lake Tribune*, 3 May 1998.

30. See Patrick Q. Mason, *What Is Mormonism? A Student's Introduction* (New York: Routledge, 2017), chap. 9.

31. See Walter E. A. van Beek, "Church Unity and the Challenge of Cultural Diversity: A View from across the Sahara," in *Directions for Mormon Studies in the Twenty-First Century*, ed. Patrick Q. Mason (Salt Lake City: University of Utah Press, 2016), 72–98.

32. 4 Nephi 1:3; see also Acts 2:44–45, 4:34–35.

33. Moses 7:18; Alma 1:30.

34. Chad Stone, Danilo Trisi, Arloc Sherman, and Jennifer Beltran, "A Guide to Statistics on Historical Trends in Income Inequality," Center on Budget and Policy Priorities, 13 January 2020, https://www.cbpp.org/research/poverty-and-inequality/a-guide-to-statistics-on-historical-trends-in-income-inequality, accessed 15 May 2020.

35. Circular of the First Presidency and Quorum of Twelve Apostles, "Zion's Co-operative Mercantile Institution," 10 July 1875, Church History Library. A similar Apostolic Circular was released the following year.

36. See Ethan R. Yorgason, *Transformation of the Mormon Culture Region* (Urbana: University of Illinois Press, 2003), chap. 3.

37. See George M. Marsden, *Fundamentalism and American Culture*, 2nd ed. (New York: Oxford University Press, 2006).

38. Bowman, *The Mormon People*, 191.

39. For a very brief introduction to Girard's theory, see https://violenceandreligion.com/mimetic-theory/, accessed 17 July 2020.

40. On developing a greater tolerance for complexity and ambiguity in understanding our religion, see Patrick Q. Mason, *Planted: Belief and Belonging in an Age of Doubt* (Provo and Salt Lake City: Neal A. Maxwell Institute for Religious Scholarship and Deseret Book Company, 2015), esp. chap. 4.

CHAPTER SIX

To Renovate the World

"Still the work has, as it were, but just begun."

This is what the Twelve Apostles declared in 1845, in an audacious proclamation addressed to the kings, presidents, governors, rulers, and people of the world. In bold, unflinching language, they announced the message of the Restoration and invited the entire world to join with them in fulfilling God's purposes. And what did God intend for his children in the modern age?

"To renovate the world—to enlighten the nations—to cover the earth with light, knowledge, truth, union, peace and love."[1]

Times have changed, but our mission hasn't. If you attach yourself to the Restoration, your charge is nothing less than "to renovate the world." The Lord and his Saints have built a sturdy foundation over the past two centuries. The Church of Jesus Christ of Latter-day Saints has never been stronger. We are people of exceptional faith, loyalty, commitment, and capability. God has endowed us with enormous gifts. Now, as we embark upon the Restoration's third century, the question is, what will we do with that endowment? How will we transform capability into consequence?[2] How will we apply our distinctive gifts for the benefit of all, "to cover the earth with light, knowledge, truth, union, peace and love"?

Rather than forcing us to choose Zion *or* the world, the Restoration challenges us to do the harder—and more rewarding—work of building Zion while *also* renovating the world. To do that, we have to relearn to love the world. To take a line from one of the *Star Wars* films, "That's how we're gonna win. Not fighting what we hate. Saving what we love."

Loving the World

"The world" is a phrase commonly heard in Latter-day Saint circles, but usually with at least a tinge of disparagement. "The world" is impure, sinful, godless, and dangerous. We are commanded in scripture to keep ourselves "unspotted from the world."[3] The pioneers' trek to the Great Basin was in many ways a retreat from a world that had frankly been rather unkind to them. They sought a place where they could practice their religion unsullied from the world as they anticipated the imminent return of Jesus. The thing is, Jesus didn't come back (yet). The world kept spinning. And it caught up with the Saints.

The Saints were forced to engage with the world, but it has been an uneasy relationship. It's like we were gawky thirteen-year-olds forced to peel ourselves off the wall and slow dance in the school gym. There was the awkwardness and embarrassment of the initial clasp—whose hands go where? But once we settled in and started to enjoy it, even venturing in a little closer, a chaperone appeared seemingly out of nowhere to ensure there was at least the width of a Book of Mormon—if not that of a full quad—between us. For much of our history, our general modes of operation vis-à-vis "the world" were risk aversion, retreat, and retrenchment, with limited forays out of the fortress church in order to gain converts, make money, play sports or music, or get elected.

And yet, "God so loved the world, that he gave his only begotten Son. . . . For God sent not his Son into the world to condemn the world; but that the world through him might be saved."[4]

God doesn't love everything that happens in this world. He especially weeps over the ways that we harm one another.[5] But *God loves the world*. He loves the world so much that he enters it, again and again and again. He entered it through Creation, he entered it through the Incarnation, he enters it through the Restoration, he enters it every day through his ongoing Atonement. God loves the world. Through loving God, we will come to love what he loves.

As we mark the Restoration's bicentennial, I think we have to admit that Latter-day Saints have yet to fully engage with the world. Engaging needn't mean wholesale acceptance—to dance is not to go home with someone and spend the night. Ours can and should be a discerning, critical relationship. But in the Restoration's third century, it's time to transform what we have traditionally treated as the specifically Latter-day Saint aspects of the Restoration into something more expansive, a vision that encompasses humanity at large—and not just by way of potential converts. With a broader sense of purpose, with greater confidence about our distinctive gifts, and with the humility that comes from knowing that there's a lot we don't yet know, we can passionately attach ourselves to the world without being subsumed by it. What might that look like?

It begins with our Thirteenth Article of Faith: "We believe all things. . . . If there is anything virtuous, lovely, or of good report or praiseworthy, we seek after these things." This is nothing if not a meditation on loving the world and a charge to embrace all the good things we find there. Naturally, we want to be selective—we don't seek after the unvirtuous, repulsive, or unworthy. But God calls us to be curious and capacious in our pursuit of truth. Brigham Young, who was hardly wishy-washy about his religion, insisted that Latter-day Saints should seek all the truth they could find, regardless of where it came from:

> It is now our duty and calling to gather up every item of truth . . . whether the infidels have it[,] the universalists . . . the Church of Rome . . . the Methodists . . . or Quakers or Shakers or the Presbyterians or the Baptists . . . every one of them have more or less truth . . . yes to the sciences of the day[,] yes to the philosophy in every nation kindred tongue and people . . . no matter how many errors they have they have a great many truths.[6]

Does the world contain dangerous falsehoods? Yes, of course. But one of the chief purposes of the Holy Ghost is to help us discern truth from error. This is precisely what the Lord told Joseph Smith when he wondered whether it was appropriate to read the apocryphal books that had been expunged from most Protestant Bibles—Maccabees, Judith, the Wisdom of Solomon, and the like. "There are many things contained therein that are true," the revelation stated, as well as "many things contained therein that are *not* true." The Lord's advice to Joseph wasn't to shield his eyes—or fail to open the book altogether—because of the risk that he might encounter error. Rather, he encouraged Joseph to read with discernment, "for the Spirit manifesteth truth; And whoso is enlightened by the Spirit shall obtain benefit."[7]

With the Spirit as our guide, the world is our school. "Things both in heaven and in the earth, and under the earth; things which have been, things which are, things which must shortly come to pass; things which are at home, things which are abroad"—it's all part of the Restoration.[8] Note that Brigham Young said we were to bring it *all* to Zion—religious truth, scientific truth, philosophical truth, it's all good. Latter-day Saints didn't come up with democracy, or women's rights, or the modern novel, or quantum physics, or modern art, or a zillion other wonderful things. No matter. We don't need to claim ownership or be at the forefront. Remember: other people have their parts of the farm which they are far more expert in cultivating. It is our privilege and responsibility simply to share in the bounteous harvest.

God endows us with a spirit of love and discernment, not fear.[9] We don't have to be afraid of the world. We don't have to be afraid about sending our children to universities or living and working in places where most of our acquaintances will not be members of our church (or any church). We might even recognize that those we thought were enemies turn out to be friends. In particular, a more expansive view of the Restoration can embrace some aspects of secularism rather than feel embattled by them. The fact is, secularism is here to stay as one of the principal conditions of the modern world. This should not fill us with dread. Latter-day Saints, of all people, should be grateful for secularism because without its bequest of disestablishment and religious freedom, there would have been no Restoration; at least, God would have had to work a lot harder or break through in another time and place. Secularism, especially of its more benign varieties, is not the enemy. It is the very air we breathe, and the foundation for modern democracy, science, and human rights.

The Restoration needs to be informed to be relevant. It cannot speak to a world that it doesn't fully understand and appreciate. God commands us to learn all "things both in heaven and earth" so we can fulfill the Restoration's mission in the world.[10] Sure, we can learn those things simply because we're supposed to, as if it's some kind of cosmic homework assignment. But God calls us to love, not just to duty. Our engagement with the world will be transformative only once we learn to love it.

Seeking a Better World

For all its goodness, however, the world isn't good enough. It is fallen. We are wanderers in a vale of tears. There is so much suffering and pain. Engaging with the world means coming face to face with its ugliness as well as its beauty. To participate in the Restoration is to strive mightily, in company with Jesus and our brothers and sisters of all faiths and no faith, "to renovate the world . . . to cover the earth with light, knowledge, truth, union, peace and love."

At the dawn of the Restoration, the Lord counseled Emma Smith to "lay aside the things of this world, and seek for the things of a better."[11] One of the Restoration's heroes, Helmuth Hübener, a sixteen-year-old German who actively opposed the Nazis and was executed for it, similarly looked forward to a "better world."[12] On this side of Christ's Second Coming, a perfect world will remain out of our reach. While the Restoration eagerly anticipates the return of Jesus, it also impels us not to wait until he comes to renovate the world. At the heart of the Restoration message is the clarion call to build Zion—here and now, not tomorrow and somewhere else.

Here is the crucial point we have too often missed: Zion is not only for the Saints. Zion is for the world. Latter-day Saints have a crucial role in envisioning and building Zion, yes, but establishing God's beloved community is never an exercise in tribalism. One of Joseph Smith's foundational revelations about the building of Zion made this clear. The last verses of Doctrine and Covenants 45 show that Zion will be the refuge of every person, from every nation under heaven, who wants peace. Zion is a multicultural, multilingual, multifaith community of people who reject the world's many forms of violence and hatred and abuse, and build instead a world dedicated to peace, love, and joy.[13] So if you seek a better world, roll up your sleeves, bring some friends, and get to work.

Imagine the building of Zion like a cross between a Habitat for Humanity project and an Extreme Home Makeover. We already have a home, so rather than building a new one, we're tasked with a massive renovation project. The bones are good—

the Architect and General Contractor knew what they were doing—but the residents have been rough on the place. There's been some pretty serious wear and tear over the years, and we're going to have to do some major remodeling to make the house sustainably livable. The project brings together ordinary people, some with no previous experience in construction. They just want to help. Everyone is going to bring a different set of talents and tools. A few of us are going to bust our thumbs because we're lousy with a hammer. That's okay. The end goal is bigger than any of the participants. What matters is that you showed up and gave it your best effort, whatever that looks like. And what results is a better house—or a better world.

Renovation Projects

Individual Latter-day Saints bring an amazingly diverse array of gifts to the table. Whatever you feel passionate about, in terms of renovating the world in your sphere of influence, go do it. But when we think what Latter-day Saints might collectively contribute to God's grand Restoration project, what might it be? Let me suggest several possibilities meant to be illustrative, not exhaustive. You'll come up with your own list of renovation projects, but here's mine.

Re-enchantment. The great sociologist Max Weber observed that one of the characteristics of modern society is "disenchantment." In place of traditional societies that are "enchanted" with supernatural beings and cosmic portent, modern societies have organized themselves around rational, secular, scientific, and bureaucratic norms. As we've noted, the Restoration is fully at home in that rational, secular, scientific world. And when a religion canonizes meeting minutes and press releases in its scriptures, as we have, you know it's comfortable with modern bureaucratic forms.[14]

While a disenchanted world can be efficient, productive, and even ethical, it is also spiritually sterile. It cannot fulfill the deepest yearnings of the human soul. In the midst of a disenchanted modernity, the Restoration offers re-enchantment. This is a modernity in which an engineer designs satellite components during the day, then returns home to pray over dinner, read scriptures with her family, and go out with the missionaries where she testifies to a complete stranger of the actual reality of God and resurrection and angels and gold plates. A modernity in which an expertly trained physician administers cutting-edge medicine, then upon request lays hands upon a person's head and invokes the powers of heaven to heal them. A modernity in which "your sons and your daughters shall prophesy, your old men shall dream dreams, your young men shall see visions"—and one of those young men will be directed by an angel to pull gold plates out of a hill, thereby ushering in God's grand era of Restoration.[15]

There are billions of people of faith on this planet, many of whom have been touched by the divine in their own way, according to their understanding.[16] But a loving God looking down from the heavens knew where and when and how modern disenchantment would proceed among his children. So he visited a boy in New York in 1820, sent him an angel three years later, and inspired him to produce a book whose origin story strains credulity and whose best self-evidence comes not from archaeology or linguistics but from prayer and revelation. God did all this "that faith also might increase in the earth."[17] Because faith matters. Anytime we increase faith in the world, or encourage others to do the same, we are doing the work of restoring enchantment in a disenchanted age.

Human identity. When our Primary children sing "I Am a Child of God," they are doing something radical. They are affirming the most important fact that every person on earth needs to know: that they are a daughter or son of a Heavenly Mother and Father. Too often we take this for granted. Maybe because we teach our three-year-old children to sing it, we think of it as somehow juvenile. In doing so, we are living far beneath our privileges. If there is one truth that the Restoration must shout from the rooftops to every man, woman, and child among every nation, kindred, tongue, and people, it is that they are children of Heavenly Parents who love them infinitely. If people aren't prepared or interested to hear about their Parents, fine—we'll simply assure them in every way we can, in whatever language they can understand, that they are of absolutely infinite worth.

In doing so, we will need to be better at affirming female identity. Again, I don't have all the answers here. But when it comes to modern questions of female equality, we've been playing with one hand tied behind our backs. A few years ago when I taught a graduate seminar on gender and Mormonism (as we then called it), my non-Latter-day Saint students were practically speechless when they found out about our doctrine of a Mother in Heaven. It was frankly one of the most attractive aspects of our religion to them. My sense is that now more than ever there is a deep yearning among the Saints—and others—to get to know their Heavenly Mother and build a connection with her. Our daughters need to know their destiny, and our sons need to know their Mother. As we enter our third century, one remarkable gift the Latter-day Saints could give would be to more fully reveal our Mother to her children around the world.[18]

Religious freedom. Unfortunately, in the United States the concept of religious freedom has gotten sucked up in partisan rancor. Religious freedom should not be a political football. It is a fundamental human right, a core foundation of the Restoration. Indeed, of all universal human rights, freedom of religion may be the one that Latter-day Saints have a special mission to protect and promote. The Book of Mormon makes clear that religious liberty is fundamental to a just society, even (or especially) to guarantee the rights of those who are critical of our faith.[19] The Doctrine and Covenants asserts that one of the essential roles of government is "the protection of all citizens in the free exercise of their religious belief."[20] The eleventh Article of Faith states it succinctly: "We claim the privilege of worshiping Almighty God according to the dictates of our own conscience, and allow all [people] the same privilege, let them worship how, where, or what they may." Our "allowance" for others should be as active as our "claim" for ourselves.

When religious freedom comes under threat, that is a genuine cause for concern. This was brought home to me a few years ago when I attended a gathering of representatives from minority religious traditions around the world. I happened to sit next to a Chinese woman who became a police officer out of an admirable desire to serve and protect her community. However, she became horrified when she saw direct evidence of the ways that her fellow law enforcement officers regularly harassed, detained, and tortured members of her own church. Stories like this are multiplied daily across the world. The 2020 report of the independent, bipartisan U.S. Commission on International Religious Freedom called out egregious abuses in fourteen "countries of particular concern," with almost twenty additional countries put on a special watchlist.[21] At the same time, many secular organizations and activists express concern about what they perceive as religious overreach in the United States, which has a history of religious majoritarianism.[22]

Some Latter-day Saints are already at the forefront of the fight for religious freedom around the globe. Brigham Young University law professor Cole Durham is widely recognized as one of the world's preeminent religious freedom experts, along with his colleagues at the International Center for Law and Religion Studies. This is a model of how Latter-day Saints can seize an issue that arises from our own theology and collective experience and then mobilize in the service of others. Our voice on behalf of religious freedom will be most powerful when it is heard not as special pleading for our own cause but rather as championing the rights of oppressed and vulnerable people everywhere—of all faiths or of no faith at all. The question is whether we will stick our neck out for others even at the risk of our own interests. We didn't do that in Germany during the Nazi era (despite the individual courage of Helmuth Hübener, as I mentioned above),[23] and we have generally been wary of antagonizing governments upon which we also rely to allow our missionaries to proselytize.

Working to extend genuine religious freedom to every one of God's children is a renovation project the world truly needs. We can't do it alone, but we can lend our voices and efforts to partner with others who feel similarly committed to this issue.

Refugees and immigrants. "Their story *is* our story, not that many years ago."[24] As area president in Europe, Elder Patrick Kearon supervised the church's relief efforts to address the refugee crisis stemming from the war in Syria as well as other conflicts in Africa and the Middle East in the mid-to-late 2010s. As Elder Kearon reminded us, Mary and Joseph and their baby Jesus were refugees. The Israelites were refugees upon fleeing pharaoh's armies. Lehi's band were refugees fleeing for their safety until they made their way to the promised land. And some early Latter-day Saints became refugees as many as four times in the space of a decade and a half. In introducing the church's "I Was a Stranger" program, Relief Society General President Linda K. Burton specifically encouraged all the women of the church to "prayerfully determine what you can do—according to your own time and circumstance—to serve the refugees living in your neighborhoods and communities."[25]

My wife Melissa felt especially moved by this counsel and the plight of refugees. With no prior experience in this area, but with a heart for both justice and compassion, she joined with a handful of other moms at our local elementary school in southern California. One of the other women was a Latter-day Saint; I'm not sure whether the others were even religious. Together they created from scratch a new nonprofit organization to assist refugee families in their transition to life in America. It was intense, emotional, and often wrenching work to accompany these struggling families on a one-on-one basis. They had their share of triumphs as well as tragedies. None of the women were paid. For their tireless and innovative work their organization was recognized with a local civic award, and they got connected to national and international leaders working in this area, including Chinese dissident artist and social activist Ai Weiwei. But the recognition wasn't the point—the people were.

Melissa has a heart for refugees partly just because she's a good person and strives to be a follower of Christ. But it's personal for her too. She comes from a proud Mexican-American family who have lived on the south Texas border for generations. On her paternal side, her ancestors were original land-grant Spanish settlers near modern-day Victoria, Texas, who then lost their lands when the "gringos" came; as they say, "We didn't cross the border, the border crossed us!" On her maternal side, her grandparents were migrant workers for much of their lives. As the family gringo, I've still never had a real conversation with her Spanish-speaking grandmother. National borders are complex things, and the politics surrounding them are divisive. But the lived experience of the De Leon and Gomez clans reinforces the church's official position that discussions about immigration should proceed first from the Christian conviction that we must love our neighbors—meaning "all of God's children, in all places, at all times"—and that we must always advocate for policies that strengthen families and keep them together.[26]

By ourselves, Latter-day Saints aren't going to solve the global refugee and immigration crises. But "their story is our story." This could be the kind of signature issue upon which we take a stand, organize our considerable resources in partnership with others, and say "never again." We can be like the good citizens of Quincy, Illinois, who took in and championed the poor, starving, desperate, victimized, and huddled Latter-day Saint families who showed up on their doorstep in the winter of 1838–39. The Restoration of God's people cannot be complete as long as any of his children languish in squalid refugee camps or immigration detention centers.

Social justice. I know that "social justice" has become a byword in many circles. That needn't be the case for Latter-day Saints. The Restoration seeks to renovate the world to make communities more just and equal. That has always been the call of the gospel, from the Hebrew prophets to the early Christians to the Latter-day Saints. We care about human society because God cares about human society. So if you don't like the term "social justice," just think about the many ways you can fulfill what the church's *General Handbook* identifies as one of the four "aspects of God's work," namely, "caring for those in need."[27]

During the bicentennial celebration of the Restoration in the April 2020 General Conference, Elder Jeffrey R. Holland powerfully preached that "the Restoration reaffirmed the foundational truth that God does work in this world." Because of this, "we *can* hope, we *should* hope, even when facing the most insurmountable odds." In 2020 that meant fighting a global pandemic. But there remain other fights:

> When we have conquered this [pandemic]—and we will—may we be equally committed to freeing the world from the virus of hunger, freeing neighborhoods and nations from the virus of poverty. May we hope for schools where children are taught—not terrified they will be shot—and for the gift of personal dignity for every child of God, unmarred by *any* form of racial, ethnic, or religious prejudice.[28]

The issues facing our society are legion, and they are daunting. But the Restoration invites us to put our shoulder to the wheel. Elder

Holland reminds us that the work of ending hunger is the work of the Restoration. The work of alleviating poverty is the work of the Restoration. The work of education is the work of the Restoration. The work of preventing violence and building peace is the work of the Restoration. The work of fighting for human dignity, racial justice, and the elimination of any form of prejudice is the work of the Restoration.

At the outset of the Restoration, the Lord commanded the Saints to "be anxiously engaged in a good cause, and do many things of their own free will, and bring to pass much righteousness."[29] What are you called to do? What is your vocation? Look around at what your community needs, and look inside at where your heart is tugging you. Do some pondering, do some praying, then go and get involved. When you work to make your community a better place, it will not be tangential to the work of the Restoration but right at the heart of it.

Community. One of the most endangered species in our modern world is community. Not the kind that exists virtually in cyberspace, but real, flesh-and-blood, face-to-face community—the kind that's actually going to a) know you're sick, and b) bring over some chicken noodle soup. For years, scholars have been observing and lamenting the loss of community in modern Western societies—a phenomenon that one sociologist famously called "bowling alone."[30] It seems that every new technological development that promises to connect us serves only to further alienate us from one another or splinter us into ever-more-fractured tribes.

Latter-day Saints have a gift and calling for community. From the very beginning, the Restoration was as much about gathering people to Zion as getting them to heaven. I know we drive each other nuts, but that's the point. It's easy to be decent to your self-selected friends. But "if you love those who love you, what reward do you have?"[31] Modern society is all about the freedom to choose: you choose your spouse, you choose your college, you choose your profession, you choose where to live, you choose which of a gazillion shows you want to watch on your choice of streaming services on your choice of mobile devices with your choice of internet providers. If you choose to affiliate with the Church of Jesus Christ of Latter-day Saints, however, you don't choose who you attend church with. Nor do you choose your church leaders at either the local or general level. They're just there, and you deal with it. This is the sociological genius of the Restoration. Most importantly, this is the Lord's laboratory of love, and this is why, as Eugene England so memorably wrote, "the church is as true as the gospel."[32]

Our church isn't the only model community in today's world, but it's an awfully good one. If we will reflect on the lessons about living in community that we learn in our wards and branches, translate them for public consumption, and then take them out into our communities, we will go a long way toward renovating the world for good.[33]

Reimagining the Future

The Restoration's fundamental mission hasn't changed since the Twelve Apostles made their proclamation in 1845. The details will differ, but the work of the Latter-day Saints in our third century will be the same as it has always been: to renovate the world, and bless the entire family of God, by adding just as much light, knowledge, truth, unity, peace, and love as we can muster.

Religion is at its most potent when it "challenges the present, and reimagines the future."[34] The world cries out in need. Heaven responds with the Restoration. God invites us not to live in a glorious past but to reimagine a better future—then work to make it a reality. Now is not the time to rest on our laurels. Latter-day Saints have an absolutely vital role to play in the modern world, but we can fulfill our mission only as we work in love and unity with one another and in partnership with others. This isn't the latest in a series of new church initiatives or programs. The purpose of the Restoration is nothing less than to restore God's people—all of God's children, not just the members of our church—to wholeness. If that doesn't take your breath away, check your pulse, because your heart isn't working.

"How vast is our purpose, how broad is our mission."[35] This line from a hymn typically sung by women in the church should be the mantra for all of us associated with the Restoration. Our broad purpose and mission beckon us out of our fortress church. We are called to be light, yeast, and salt to elevate and transform the world. Our Heavenly Parents want to restore all their children to happiness and peace and flourishing, in this life and the next. They have given us a special mission to alleviate the pain and suffering of the marginalized, the outcast, the voiceless, and the abused and to use our church community to do so. We will best fulfill this mission when we discard the excess baggage that has been weighing us down and catch a vision of the new work that God is doing in the world today.

Our Father and Mother love the world. They will restore their people. They sent their Son to redeem us. Now they're asking for us to join them in the glorious work we call the Restoration.

Are you in?

NOTES

1. Proclamation of the Twelve Apostles of the Church of Jesus Christ of Latter-day Saints (New York, 1845), 4–5, available online at https://contentdm.lib.byu.edu/digital/collection/NCMP1820-1846/id/2818/.

2. See Richard Bushman, "Embracing a 'Radiant' Mormonism," *Deseret News*, 16 November 2017, https://www.deseret.com/2017/11/16/20623103/richard-bushman-embracing-a-radiant-mormonism, accessed 30 May 2020.

3. James 1:27; Doctrine and Covenants 59:9.

4. John 3:16–17.

5. Moses 7:28–40.

6. Brigham Young discourse, 9 October 1959, transcription available at https://catalog.churchofjesuschrist.org/assets?id=4108f87d-dcdc-4019-8c54-2984d06a63e7&crate=0&index=0, accessed 17 July 2020; see also *Journal of Discourses* 7:283–84.

7. Doctrine and Covenants 91:1–5, emphasis added.

8. Doctrine and Covenants 88:79.

9. See 2 Timothy 1:7.

10. Doctrine and Covenants 88:79–80; see also 93:53.

11. Doctrine and Covenants 25:10.

12. Blair R. Holmes and Alan F. Keele, comp., trans., and ed., *When Truth Was Treason: German Youth against Hitler* (Urbana: University of Illinois Press, 1995), 240.

13. See Doctrine and Covenants 45:66–71.

14. See Doctrine and Covenants 102; Official Declaration 2.

15. Joel 2:28; see also Joseph Smith-History 1:41.

16. See 2 Nephi 31:3.

17. Doctrine and Covenants 1:21.

18. Helpful resources include David L. Paulsen and Martin Pulido, "'A Mother There': A Survey of Historical Teachings about Mother in Heaven," *BYU Studies* 50:1 (2011): 70–97; MacArthur Krishna and Bethany Brady Spalding, *A Girl's Guide to Heavenly Mother* (Portland, OR: D Street Press, 2020).

19. See Alma 1:17.

20. Doctrine and Covenants 134:7.

21. https://www.uscirf.gov/reports-briefs/annual-report/2020-annual-report.

22. See David Sehat, *The Myth of American Religious Freedom* (New York: Oxford University Press, 2011); Tisa Wenger, *Religious Freedom: The*

Contested History of an American Ideal (Chapel Hill: University of North Carolina Press, 2017).

23. See David Conley Nelson, *Moroni and the Swastika: Mormons in Nazi Germany* (Norman: University of Oklahoma Press, 2015).

24. Patrick Kearon, "Refuge from the Storm," April 2016 General Conference.

25. Linda K. Burton, "I Was a Stranger," April 2016 General Conference.

26. https://newsroom.churchofjesuschrist.org/official-statement/immigration.

27. *General Handbook: Serving in The Church of Jesus Christ of Latter-day Saints* (Salt Lake City: The Church of Jesus Christ of Latter-day Saints, 2020), 1.2. See also Sharon Eubank, "And the Lord Called His People Zion," *Ensign* (March 2020).

28. Jeffrey R. Holland, "A Perfect Brightness of Hope," April 2020 General Conference.

29. Doctrine and Covenants 58:27.

30. Robert D. Putnam, *Bowling Alone: The Collapse and Revival of American Community* (New York: Touchstone Books, 2001).

31. Matthew 5:46 (NRSV).

32. Eugene England, "Why the Church Is as True as the Gospel," *Sunstone* 10:10 (1986): 30–36; republished with additional material in *Sunstone* (June 1999): 61–69, also available at https://www.eugeneengland.org/why-the-church-is-as-true-as-the-gospel. See also Patrick Q. Mason, *Planted: Belief and Belonging in an Age of Doubt* (Salt Lake City and Provo: Deseret Book and Neal A. Maxwell Institute for Religious Scholarship, 2015), chap. 8.

33. See "The King's Good Servant—But God's First: Terryl Givens with Thomas Griffith," Faith Matters, March 15, 2020, https://faithmaters.org/the-kings-good-servant-but-gods-first-terryl-givens-with-thomas-griffith/; Thomas B. Griffith, "A Mormon Approach to Politics," *BYU Studies* 52:1 (2013): 125–135.

34. Tara Isabella Burton, "Christianity Gets Weird," *New York Times*, 8 May 2020, https://www.nytimes.com/2020/05/08/opinion/sunday/weird-christians.html.

35. "As Sisters in Zion," *Hymns* (Salt Lake City: The Church of Jesus Christ of Latter-day Saints, 1985), #309.

APPENDIX

A Restoration Manifesto

On November 1, 1831, Joseph Smith received a revelation at a church conference held in Hiram, Ohio, in which the elders were discussing the preparation of a Book of Commandments—a compendium of teachings and revelations to the prophet Joseph Smith. The Lord sent a message through Joseph and designated that it should be placed at the opening of the book as its "preface." The revelation was published as Chapter 1 of the Book of Commandments and has appeared as Section 1 in every succeeding edition of the Doctrine and Covenants.[1]

Although the revelation never uses the word "restoration," it offers a compelling vision of what God intends to accomplish in today's world. After an initial call to attention, it diagnoses some of modern society's spiritual pitfalls, affirms the prophetic calling of Joseph Smith, and outlines four purposes for the Restoration.

As such, D&C 1 is as close to a divine manifesto for the Restoration as we have.

Maybe you've read this section a hundred times; maybe it's entirely new to you. Either way, I'd like to ask you to look with fresh eyes at God's words to our modern world. What follows here is, to borrow a term and a method from Latter-day Saint theologian Adam Miller, an "urgent paraphrase" of this revealed scripture.[2] I haven't improved upon the original; undoubtedly the opposite is true. If this is successful, it should take you back to the actual text to discover God's voice, fired with a sense of urgency and mission about the nature and purpose of the Restoration and what you are called to do as part of it.

*

Listen up!

Everyone, pay attention! Church members, I'm talking to you. Everyone else, in whatever corner of the world you may live in, I'm talking to you too. I've been watching you all, and have a few things to say, so gather 'round and listen.

My voice and my word are for everyone, no exceptions. Eventually, every one of my children will see that I am God. Every ear will hear my voice, and every heart will be penetrated by my Spirit. Those who resist my love will eventually be filled with regret. And those who think they can do evil in secret will be exposed for who and what they really are.

When you hear my voice, consider it a loving but stern warning. I'm posting notice for every person on earth. Some people will hear my voice directly, but most will hear it from my followers whom I have asked to help spread the message. Time is short; there's not a moment to waste. My followers understand this, so they're out spreading the word. I've told them to do it, and it's going to get done—one way or the other, sooner or later. When they share the good news of Jesus Christ with you, they do it in my name and with my authority. They'll bring with them new scriptures and new revelations—including this one—that are meant for all of my children around the world. I know this will produce anxiety, even fear, among many of you when you realize that I'm serious. But everything I talk about here is happening or going to happen. This is real.

Recall what Jesus taught: You will be judged by the way you have judged your fellow humans. Your life will be measured in the same way that you have measured others. You are accountable for who and what you are. The way you respond to the gospel will confirm whether you're humble and submissive or stubborn and rebellious. You have the freedom to choose what to believe and do, but you can't choose the consequences. It's the law of the harvest—just as you sow you shall reap.

I love you. That's why I'm speaking to every one of you, near and far, to the ends of the earth, if you'll only listen. *Listen!* There's no time to wait. The consequences of your actions are already here. If I sound angry, it's because I am. You haven't listened to me, you haven't listened to my followers, you haven't listened to the prophets and apostles I've been sending for millennia now. When will you get the picture? Unless you listen—now—you're going to lose out and be cut off from the community that will ultimately sustain you.

People, get ready.

I've been calling my children to repentance since the beginning. But there's a special set of problems with the modern world. You've walked away from law. You've become so casual and dismissive of ritual that you don't even understand its power anymore. You've abandoned the covenant I gave to Abraham—that I would be your God, and you would be my people. You've forgotten the whole purpose of that covenant—to unite the whole human family in one, as children of a Heavenly Mother and Father with a destiny to become like them.

In place of this covenant of love and belonging, you've decided to go your own way. You scoff at old-fashioned terms like "righteousness." You want to set your own rules. You grow less interested in me by the hour. Instead, you follow the Gospel of I: first iPads and iPhones, and now iProphets and iReligion. You're idol worshippers, plain and simple. Money, sex, drugs, McMansions, stock portfolios, technology, ideologies, politics, "likes." You've created a golden calf out of your own ego. You've become captives to your own desires. You're turning the whole world into the Las Vegas Strip—a mirage, a sham, a testament to decadence and sensation and self-worship. You think you can build a society like this, but it's impossible. It's not sustainable. You can't go on living like this. It seems great now, but it will all come tumbling down.

What you're doing with the world and yourselves is nothing short of a calamity. A disaster. A catastrophe. It's tragic, and it breaks my heart.

You have a big problem on your hands. I've got a solution. To counter your self-worship, I called a new messenger for a new age: Joseph Smith Jr. That's right—a poor farm boy whose many weaknesses are apparent for anyone to see. Does that surprise you? Read your Bible. I spoke to Joseph straight from heaven and gave him commandments to give to you. But for heaven's sake, don't make an idol of Joseph too—this story isn't about him. I also spoke to plenty of others and made them messengers of my word. I could have used more accomplished, more polished, more impressive means, but I wanted to prove a point to you. It's the "weak" things of this world that will break down your perception of what's "mighty" and "strong." Stop the self-worship!

To use your utilitarian language, what are my "objectives" here? It's simple. Four things:

First, that every man, woman, and child will speak in the name of Jesus. This means not only speaking reverently of Jesus Christ, your Lord and Savior, but that everything you breathe out into the world will be filtered through his holy name. To take on and speak in the name of Jesus is to walk in the Way of Truth and Life.

Second, that faith will increase throughout the world. Yes, of course that means I want more of my children in relationship with me and not being seduced by materialism and atheism. But on a deeper level, I mean trust. Trust in my love and my law. And also trust one another enough to build Zion together.

Third, that my everlasting covenant will be (re-)established. The bonds of love must be extended among all women, men, and children (what my servants in the civil rights movement called the "beloved community"). Not just now, but across the generations, both past and future. The hearts of the children must turn to the ancestors, and in turn you must think about your impact on descendants yet unborn. Your calling is to unite all humanity as the family of God that it is.

Fourth, that the good news of my love will be spread to all the world. Don't leave anyone out. Don't be afraid to speak up for truth and love even in the public square. You may feel weak or feel that your message is too simple, but see #2 above: have faith. Those who think they are powerful, those in positions of authority, those who are deeply ensnared in self-worship, are the ones who need to hear this message the most.

Look, I'm God, and you're not. I'm trying to communicate with you in language that you'll comprehend. That's always true of how I work with my servants. I speak with them in their own language, in ways that they can understand even in their weakness. When they make mistakes—and they do—I let it be known. When they truly seek wisdom, I give it to them. When my servants sin—and they do (again, read the Bible)—I chastise them so they can learn and change and do better the next time. But when they are humble, that's when they are strong. That's when they are blessed. That's when, every so often, they are prepared for me to send down knowledge like manna from heaven.

These principles apply to Joseph Smith and all my other servants in the modern age. After he received the gold plates, Joseph had power to translate the Book of Mormon only through my mercy and power. The same is true of the saints who laid the foundation of the Church of Jesus Christ. They had power to do so—to bring the church out of obscurity and into the light of day where everyone can see it—insofar as they sought forgiveness and relied on me. The Church of Jesus Christ is the only true and living church. That's not because of any great virtues of its individual members, all of whom are in need of repentance, but because collectively the church points people to salvation in Christ and the building of Zion. I simply can't overlook the many things you do to separate yourself from me. Those who remain enmeshed in sin drive away my Spirit until, if they don't turn around, they lose the light I've given them; at a certain point they just forget how to hear and respond to spiritual things. That's what sin is—the act and state of alienating yourself from me and my love. So yes, I'm well pleased with the church in a collective sense, precisely because it is a gift I have given the world as part of my answer to the calamity of modern self-worship. But don't get full of yourselves just because you happen to be in the club—which is so exclusive that I want everyone to become a member!

Please listen to me when I tell you that I want nothing more than for everyone to know and embrace the good news of redemption. I love all my children equally; I don't privilege one person or group over any other. I want every man, woman, and child to realize how urgent this is. The end isn't here yet, but it's coming soon. I can't promise you perpetual peace in these troubling times. The world you thought you were building for yourself will be claimed as part of the devil's dominions. But you can always find refuge in me. Trust that I have power to protect those who come to me. The day of reckoning for this sin-sick age is coming, so you need to choose what kind of world you want.

Search my word as recorded in modern scripture. The revelations are true. The prophecies and promises I have given will all be fulfilled. Trust me. I don't need to justify the things I've said to you. Everything you think you know will come and go. The world you have so carefully cultivated will fade away. But my word will not. My promises will not. My love never fails. If it's truly the gospel of Jesus Christ, it doesn't matter whether you hear it straight from me or from one of my servants. The prophecies and promises are true, and you need to respond just the same.

You can know that what I'm saying is true because the Spirit will bear witness of it to your soul. You can rely on that truth forever. Amen.

NOTES

1. In preparing this paraphrase, I referred to the first printed version of the revelation, published as Chapter 1 in the 1833 Book of Commandments, reprinted in Robin Scott Jensen, Richard E. Turley Jr., and Riley M. Lorimer, eds., *Revelations and Translations, Volume 2: Published Revelations*, vol. 2 of the Revelations and Translations series of The Joseph Smith Papers, ed. Dean C. Jessee, Ronald K. Esplin, and Richard Lyman Bushman (Salt Lake City: Church Historian's Press, 2011), 3–6.

2. Adam S. Miller, *Grace Is Not God's Backup Plan: An Urgent Paraphrase of Paul's Letter to the Romans* (self-published, 2015). In addition to taking his phrase, I'm also adopting Miller's method: "I've rendered [the text] with a relatively free hand. . . . Rather than worry over the letter of the text, my goal has been to illuminate the large scale patterns that structure it. With little hesitation, I've sacrificed some concern for details to a more urgent need for persuasion and clarity. At several points, I've cut some details for the sake of fluidity. At other points, I've expanded the material with additional explanation. Overall, I've purposely adopted a brisk, contemporary idiom" (6).

Acknowledgments

The last social engagement that Melissa and I had before the COVID-19 pandemic forced us into social isolation was a dinner with Bill and Susan Turnbull and Terryl Givens in which Bill pitched the idea of a new book series to be published by Faith Matters. I had been mulling over and making notes on much of the material that appears here, originally thinking these ideas would find their way into one or two longer books. Bill is persuasive, though, and he convinced me that one short book might be the better approach. Readers will no doubt appreciate Bill's insistence on a limited word count.

Thanks to Bill and David Turnbull for having the vision and then investing in the creation and expansion of Faith Matters. The quality of my conversations with these remarkable brothers has shaped much of what appears here, not least their vision of an expansive Restoration that can and must be in conversation with the wider world. It's refreshing to rub shoulders with people so passionately dedicated to the old-fashioned notion that ideas matter—for everyone, not just pointy-headed intellectuals.

The definition of a true friend is someone who says yes when you send them an e-mail out of the blue saying, "I just wrote a book. Will you read the first draft?" Sincere thanks to Gary Anderson, Rob Daines, Tom Griffith, Melissa Inouye, and

Luisa Perkins, whose cheers encouraged me and gentle critiques corrected me.

If this book is halfway decent, it's because I had two of the world's best readers and editors poring over it. Jana Riess is a phenomenal editor who improved my writing on virtually every page. Every author (and reader) should be so lucky as to have someone like Jana in their corner. And I'm incredibly fortunate to have a best friend and spouse who is a voracious reader and deep thinker and will always let me know when my ideas need some work or my writing doesn't make any sense. When the book passed muster with Melissa, then I knew it was ready for print. Thank you for everything, my love.